W9-DBQ-295

FOREIGN
INTERVENTION
&
GLOBAL
SECURITY

IDEAS in CONFLICT

Gary E. McCuen

publications inc.

411 Mallalieu Drive
Hudson, Wisconsin 54016
Phone (715) 386-7113

Illustration and Photo Credits

Kirk Anderson 104; Steven Benson 86; Darren Brettingen 91; Carol & Simpson 142; Center for Defense Information 117; Bob Gorrell 161; Joe Heller 146; Mike Keefe 128; Jeff MacNelly 35, 151; Jim Morin 47; Mike Ramirez 81, 112; Steve Sack 41, 97, 157; Bill Sanders 138; Ben Sargent 26; Wayne Stayskal 11; Dale Stephanos 61; U.S. Department of Defense 122; Richard Wright 16, 53, 66, 75.

© 1995 by Gary E. McCuen Publications, Inc.
411 Mallalieu Drive, Hudson, Wisconsin 54016

(715) 386-7113

International Standard Book Number
ISBN 0-86596-097-6
Printed in the United States of America

CONTENTS

Chapter 3 INTERVENTION AND GLOBAL SECURITY

Chapter 4 MILITARISM AND THE ARMS TRADE

Chapter 5 THE UNITED NATIONS & WORLD ORDER

REASONING SKILL DEVELOPMENT

These activities may be used as individualized study guides for students in libraries and resource centers or as discussion catalysts in small group and classroom discussions.

IDEAS in CONFLICT

This series features ideas in conflict on political, social, and moral issues. It presents counterpoints, debates, opinions, commentary, and analysis for use in libraries and classrooms. Each title in the series uses one or more of the following basic elements:

Introductions that present an issue overview giving historic background and/or a description of the controversy.

Counterpoints and debates carefully chosen from publications, books, and position papers on the political right and left to help librarians and teachers respond to requests that treatment of public issues be fair and balanced.

Symposiums and forums that go beyond debates that can polarize and oversimplify. These present commentary from across the political spectrum that reflect how complex issues attract many shades of opinion.

A *global* emphasis with foreign perspectives and surveys on various moral questions and political issues that will help readers to place subject matter in a less culture-bound and ethnocentric frame of reference. In an ever-shrinking and interdependent world, understanding and cooperation are essential. Many issues are global in nature and can be effectively dealt with only by common efforts and international understanding.

Reasoning skill study guides and discussion activities provide ready-made tools for helping with critical reading and evaluation of content. The guides and activities deal with one or more of the following:

RECOGNIZING AUTHOR'S POINT OF VIEW

INTERPRETING EDITORIAL CARTOONS

VALUES IN CONFLICT

WHAT IS EDITORIAL BIAS?

WHAT IS SEX BIAS?

WHAT IS POLITICAL BIAS?

WHAT IS ETHNOCENTRIC BIAS?

WHAT IS RACE BIAS?

WHAT IS RELIGIOUS BIAS?

*From across **the political spectrum** varied sources are presented for research projects and classroom discussions. Diverse opinions in the series come from magazines, newspapers, syndicated columnists, books, political speeches, foreign nations, and position papers by corporations and nonprofit institutions.*

About the Editor

Gary E. McCuen is an editor and publisher of anthologies for public libraries and curriculum materials for schools. Over the past years his publications have specialized in social, moral and political conflict. They include books, pamphlets, cassettes, tabloids, filmstrips and simulation games, many of them designed from his curriculums during 11 years of teaching junior and senior high school social studies. At present he is the editor and publisher of the *Ideas in Conflict* series.

CHAPTER 1

MILITARY INTERVENTION: HISTORY AND OVERVIEW

1   MILITARY INTERVENTION: HISTORY AND OVERVIEW

WHY NATIONS INTERVENE: AN OVERVIEW

Michael R. Beschloss

Michael R. Beschloss is an historian from Washington, D.C. He made the following comments before the Senate Foreign Relations Committee.

Points to Consider:

1. What two foreign policy controversies continue throughout all of American history?

2. Compare and contrast the "three legacies of Vietnam."

3. Discuss how Presidential power was systematically reduced.

4. How did the President justify military intervention in the Persian Gulf War?

5. What role did the U.N. play in the Persian Gulf War?

Excerpted from congressional testimony by Michael R. Beschloss before the Senate Foreign Relations Committee, February 10, 1994.

First, who makes decisions about foreign policy and use of force—the President or Congress? Second, how much should our actions in the world be based on the idealism about human rights and other values that are uniquely American?

There is a tendency in American history for each generation to believe that the difficult issues it confronts are entirely new. This is nowhere more true than in American diplomacy. When William McKinley and the Congress dealt with Spain, when Woodrow Wilson, Franklin Roosevelt and Harry Truman and later Congresses responded to world-encompassing challenges, they took actions that forever redefined the way America would relate to the rest of the world. The same is true today as this Congress and President Clinton grapple with problems like Bosnia, Somalia, Haiti and the former Soviet Union.

However new these perils may seem to Americans, history can provide context. In 1994, we are making decisions about foreign policy and the use of force in the same system and the same tradition that George Washington did in 1789. Key to this are two controversies that run through the entire two centuries of American history. First, who makes decisions about foreign policy and use of force—the President or Congress? Second, how much should our actions in the world be based on the idealism about human rights and other values that are uniquely American? How much should they be based on an unvarnished assessment of interests such as raw power politics and world economic competition? At turning points in our diplomacy like 1898, 1917, 1941 and 1946, these questions were vital. They should be just as influential today as Congress contemplates standards for commitment of U.S. forces abroad in the world after the Cold War.

This century, America's first as a superpower, has seen great swings in the pendulum between Presidential and Congressional authority in our foreign and military affairs. The boost to Presidential influence brought by President McKinley's victory in the Spanish-American War led to President Wilson's success in taking the nation into the First World War. When American attitudes toward that adventure soured in the 1920s and 1930s, Congress strove to such a degree to constrain Presidential power that in 1937, the House only narrowly rejected the Ludlow Amendment, which would have required a national referendum

"WE MUST BE GOING TO WAR... WE'RE NOT ARMED HEAVILY ENOUGH FOR A PEACE-KEEPING MISSION!"

Reprinted by permission: **Tribune Media Services**.

of all Americans to make war, except in case of invasion. The imperative of winning the Second World War and the Cold War with its danger of nuclear conflict caused Congress to cede extraordinary power to the Executive Branch. That extraordinary power allowed Presidents Kennedy, Johnson and Nixon to wage an undeclared war in Indochina for a decade.

THREE LEGACIES

Vietnam left three legacies that shape the environment we live in today. First, never again would Congress allow a President to use American force abroad for so long and with so few constraints. Congress put this determination into law with the imperfect instrument of the War Powers Act, and it tightened the leash on the Executive Branch as it pondered use of force in a host of other ways. Questioning in public hearings became tougher. Senators and Congressmen demanded more serious consultation before policies were established. Never again would Congress tolerate a scene such as that in the Cabinet Room at the White House in October 1962, when John Kennedy informed the Chairman of this Committee, Senator Fulbright, and other Congressional leaders—he did not consult them—on his plans to blockade Cuba—legally, an act of war—only ninety minutes

11

before he told the world.

A second residue of Vietnam is that both Congress and the American people are more skeptical than ever of what Presidents say to justify the use of force. Cloaking *Realpolitik* in noble rhetoric is an old Presidential practice. In 1900, when President McKinley sent 5000 U.S. troops to China, he insisted that his motive was protection of American lives and property. Actually, his real purpose was to help an international coalition invade Beijing and suppress the Boxer Rebellion. During the Vietnam War, the three Presidents concerned never satisfactorily explained to Americans what was at stake that was so important as to merit the expenditure of so much American blood and treasure. Was Indochina a vital theater in the Cold War? Were we there to show that we could not lose a war? To this day, Secretary of State Dean Rusk insists that the reason we were in Vietnam was to fulfill an obligation under the Southeast Asia Treaty Organization.

A third legacy of Vietnam is that, barring invasion of the North American landmass, our citizens are unlikely to tolerate the shedding of a great deal of American blood for a long period of time— even for a cause they are convinced is just. The conflict in Indochina so sensitized Americans to the human costs of war to their fellow citizens that they were predisposed against any costly use of force. This has been exacerbated by the presence of television. Franklin Roosevelt could prosecute the entire American effort in the Second World War without worrying that dispiriting pictures of American soldiers maimed or killed would appear on newspaper front pages or newsreel screens. L.B.J. could not do the same about the pictures of carnage in Vietnam.

PUBLIC SUSPICION

What I have called the three legacies of Vietnam—reduced Presidential power in foreign and military affairs, a new public suspiciousness and an American people unwilling to let U.S. involvement in a foreign conflict drag on—have abided fairly consistently over the past two decades. Since the moment our helicopters left our embassy in Saigon, when Presidents have felt they needed to use force, they have done so with strong attention to the new realities. The result has been a new kind of little war— shaping use of force so that it is brief and relatively inexpensive in American lives.

By declaring that Saddam's aggression would not stand, George

Bush committed the United States to using force to win the most towering U.S. military objective since the fall of Saigon. When that goal was accomplished, President Bush declared that the "Vietnam syndrome" was over, perhaps implying that Presidents and Congresses of the future might commit American troops abroad in a manner resembling the grand age of World War II (to which he frequently referred as a precedent for the Gulf) and the Cold War. I would argue that the Persian Gulf War was not a departure from U.S. military operations like Grenada and Panama. It was a much larger variant with many of the same defining qualities—the finely-calibrated effort to get in and out as quickly as possible, with overwhelming American force and as little loss as possible of American lives. Had victory taken two years instead of six weeks, with American casualties approaching the tens of thousands rumored in the runup to that war, it would almost certainly been judged a failure and caused even greater constraints to be placed on use of force by American Presidents in the future.

A U.N. COALITION

One aspect of the Gulf War, however, was a pathbreaking effort. This was Mr. Bush's insistence on waging war by coalition under U.N. auspices. By 1990, this was possible thanks to the end of the Cold War, but another Chief Executive might not have been so sensitive to the need to establish precedents for the post-Cold War world. For a President who was so dismissive of multilateralism during the 1988 campaign, George Bush made it much more difficult for later Presidents to operate as autonomously as

13

Ronald Reagan had on Grenada and Libya.

I close by touching for a moment on the tragedy in Bosnia. If the Persian Gulf can be said to have been a nearly perfect theater for use of force within what I have described as the severe constraints imposed on American Presidents and Congresses in the post-Vietnam, post-Cold War world, Bosnia has been close to being the opposite. What the history of the last twenty years and indeed the last two centuries suggests is that if Congress and the President decide to act militarily in a major fashion, it will be imperative that our leadership take with ultimate seriousness the duty to educate the American people about the full range of moral and strategic stakes involved, to gain their assent in advance and to do the same with our allies. That is a difficult job. Within the American system, it would inevitably take political attention and energy away from other issues that are urgent to Americans. If America acts without it, future generations are likely to be even more disinclined to project American power in the world when necessary. Only if America acts with its people convinced of the rightness of the cause can use of force in central Europe have a prospect of being judged a success.

MILITARY INTERVENTION:
HISTORY AND OVERVIEW

THE WAR POWERS RESOLUTION:
AN OVERVIEW

Tom Lantos

Tom Lantos is a Democratic Congressman from California. He is the Chairman of the Senate Foreign Relations Subcommittee on International Security, International Organizations and Human Rights.

Points to Consider:

1. What was the purpose of the War Powers Act adopted by Congress?

2. Discuss what led up to the discord between the Executive and Legislative branches of government.

3. List and explain the three central elements of the War Powers Resolution.

Excerpted from comments by Congressman Tom Lantos before the Senate Foreign Relations Subcommittee on International Security, International Organizations and Human Rights, May 23, 1994.

AN EMERGENCY
CALL FROM
KUWAIT, SIR...

Cartoon by Richard Wright.

The executive cannot simply inform Members of Congress of its intention to use military force. Notification is not consultation. Consultation requires dialogue.

On November 7, 1973, Congress enacted the War Powers Resolution (Public Law 93-148) over the veto of President Richard M. Nixon. The War Powers Resolution was adopted by Congress, despite the vigorous opposition of the executive branch. The Constitution specifies that only the Congress has the authority "to declare war," "to raise and support Armies," and "to provide and maintain a Navy" (Article I, section 8, clauses 11, 12, and 13). At the same time, however, the President is "Commander in Chief of the Army and Navy of the United States" (Article II, section 2, clause 1). This shared authority over our nation's military forces has been a source of conflict between the executive and legislative branches of our government at many times in our nation's history. The War Powers Resolution is an attempt to stipulate the constitutional procedures that the President and Congress should follow in order to commit the armed forces of the United States to military action abroad, and it provides that the two branches should be partners acting together, not adversaries in conflict.

CONSULTING WITH CONGRESS

The President in every possible instance shall consult with Congress before introducing United States Armed Forces into hostilities or into situations where imminent involvement in hostilities is clearly indicated by the circumstances, and after every such introduction shall consult regularly with the Congress until United States Armed Forces are no longer engaged in hostilities or have been removed from such situations.

Excerpted from a publication, "The War Powers Resolution" by the House Foreign Affairs Subcommittee on International Security, International Organizations and Human Rights, May 1994.

DISCORD

The initial sources of discord between the executive and legislative branches, which led to the adoption of the War Powers Resolution in 1973, were differences over the appropriate United States policy toward Vietnam and other countries of South East Asia. Since the enactment of the War Powers Resolution—and particularly since the end of the Cold War—the commitment of U.S. military forces abroad has increasingly involved the use of our armed forces in connection with multilateral peace-keeping and peace-enforcing operations, sometimes under the auspices of the United Nations or other international organizations.

The War Powers Resolution consists of three central elements. First, it requires the President to make every effort to consult with the Congress in advance of any decision to introduce the armed forces of the United States into hostilities or into situations in which hostilities are imminent, unless there has been a declaration of war or specific authorization by Congress. Second, it requires the President to report to Congress within 48 hours of the time that U.S. armed forces become involved in combat or of the time that the President becomes aware that hostilities involving U.S. forces are imminent. Third, it requires the Congress to authorize the deployment of U.S. armed forces within sixty days of the report's submission.

In the aftermath of the involvement of U.S. military forces under United Nations auspices in Somalia to facilitate the distribution of humanitarian assistance and to help deal with the breakdown of civil authority in that country, new questions have been raised about the adequacy of the War Powers Resolution and the mechanisms for consultations between the executive and legislative branches of our government on the commitment of U.S. military forces abroad.

A number of world events have taken place since May 1988 in which U.S. military forces have been involved in hostilities: military action in the Persian Gulf in the summer of 1988; in Panama in December 1989; in Liberia in 1990; in Somalia in 1992 and 1993; in the former Yugoslavia in 1993 and 1994, and in Haiti and Rwanda in 1994. The most significant use of U.S. military power since the adoption of the War Powers Resolution was the U.S. led military action against Iraq following Iraq's invasion of Kuwait in 1990.

3   MILITARY INTERVENTION: HISTORY AND OVERVIEW

CONGRESS DOES NOT HAVE EXCLUSIVE WAR POWERS

Richard Nixon

President Richard Nixon wrote the following statement to justify his veto of the War Powers Resolution enacted by Congress on November 7, 1973.

Points to Consider:

1. List any concerns President Nixon had regarding restrictions the President faces when Congress asserts its role in foreign affairs.

2. Evaluate the effects of the House Joint Resolution 542. Explain President Nixon's opinion on the constitutionality of these provisions.

3. According to President Nixon, how would the House Joint Resolution 542 undercut the ability of the United States to act as an effective influence for peace?

4. How important is positive Congressional action when discussing foreign policy questions?

5. What does President Nixon mean when he describes positive Congressional action in foreign policy?

Excerpted from a written statement made by former President Richard Nixon explaining his veto of the War Powers Act of 1973.

I am particularly disturbed by the fact that certain of the President's constitutional powers as Commander in Chief would terminate automatically under this resolution.

TO THE HOUSE OF REPRESENTATIVES:

I hereby return without my approval House Joint Resolution 542—the War Powers Resolution. While I am in accord with the desire of the Congress to assert its proper role in the conduct of our foreign affairs, the restrictions which this resolution would impose upon the authority of the President are both unconstitutional and dangerous to the best interests of our Nation.

The proper roles of the Congress and the Executive in the conduct of foreign affairs have been debated since the founding of our country. Only recently, however, has there been a serious challenge to the wisdom of the Founding Fathers in choosing not to draw a precise and detailed line of demarcation between the foreign policy powers of the two branches.

The Founding Fathers understood the impossibility of foreseeing every contingency that might arise in this complex area. They acknowledged the need for flexibility in responding to changing circumstances. They recognized that foreign policy decisions must be made through close cooperation between the two branches and not through rigidly codified procedures.

These principles remain as valid today as they were when our Constitution was written. Yet House Joint Resolution 542 would violate those principles by defining the President's powers in ways which would strictly limit his constitutional authority.

CLEARLY UNCONSTITUTIONAL

House Joint Resolution 542 would attempt to take away, by a mere legislative act, authorities which the President has properly exercised under the Constitution for almost 200 years. One of its provisions would automatically cut off certain authorities after sixty days unless the Congress extended them. Another would allow the Congress to eliminate certain authorities merely by the passage of a concurrent resolution—an action which does not normally have the force of law, since it denies the President his constitutional role in approving legislation.

I believe that both these provisions are unconstitutional. The only way in which the constitutional powers of a branch of the Government can be altered is by amending the Constitution—and any attempt to make such alterations by legislation alone is clearly without force.

UNDERMINING OUR FOREIGN POLICY

While I firmly believe that a veto of House Joint Resolution 542 is warranted solely on constitutional grounds, I am also deeply disturbed by the practical consequences of this resolution. For it would seriously undermine this Nation's ability to act decisively and convincingly in times of international crisis. As a result, the confidence of our allies in our ability to assist them could be diminished and the respect of our adversaries for our deterrent posture could decline. A permanent and substantial element of unpredictability would be injected into the world's assessment of American behavior, further increasing the likelihood of miscalculation and war.

If this resolution had been in operation, America's effective response to a variety of challenges in recent years would have been vastly complicated or even made impossible. We may well have been unable to respond in the way we did during the Berlin crisis of 1961, the Cuban missile crisis of 1962, the Congo rescue operation of 1964, and the Jordanian crisis of 1970—to mention just a few examples. In addition, our recent actions to bring about a peaceful settlement of the hostilities in the Middle East would have been seriously impaired if this resolution had been in force.

While all the specific consequences of House Joint Resolution 542 cannot yet be predicted, it is clear that it would undercut the ability of the United States to act as an effective influence for peace. For example, the provision automatically cutting off certain authorities after 60 days unless they are extended by the Congress could work to prolong or intensify a crisis. Until the Congress suspended the deadline, there would be at least a chance of United States withdrawal and an adversary would be tempted therefore to postpone serious negotiations until the 60 days were up. Only after the Congress acted would there be a strong incentive for an adversary to negotiate. In addition, the very existence of a deadline could lead to an escalation of hostilities in order to achieve certain objectives before the 60 days expired.

21

FAILURE TO REQUIRE POSITIVE CONGRESSIONAL ACTION

I am particularly disturbed by the fact that certain of the President's constitutional powers as Commander in Chief of the Armed Forces would terminate automatically under this resolution 60 days after they were invoked. No overt Congressional action would be required to cut off these powers—they would disappear automatically unless the Congress extended them. In effect, the Congress is here attempting to increase its policymaking role through a provision which requires it to take absolutely no action at all.

In my view, the proper way for the Congress to make known its will on such foreign policy questions is through a positive action, with full debate on the merits of the issue and with each member taking the responsibility of casting a yes or no vote after considering those merits. The authorization and appropriations process represents one of the ways in which such influence can be exercised. I do not, however, believe that the Congress can responsibly contribute its considered, collective judgment on such grave questions without full debate and without a yes or no vote. Yet this is precisely what the joint resolution would allow. It would give every future Congress the ability to handcuff every future President merely by doing nothing and sitting still. In my view, one cannot become a responsible partner unless one is prepared to take responsible action.

COOPERATION

The responsible and effective exercise of the war powers requires the fullest cooperation between the Congress and the

Executive and the prudent fulfillment by each branch of its constitutional responsibilities. House Joint Resolution 542 includes certain constructive measures which would foster this process by enhancing the flow of information from the executive branch to the Congress.

This Administration is dedicated to strengthening cooperation between the Congress and the President in the conduct of foreign affairs and to preserving the constitutional prerogatives of both branches of our Government. I know that the Congress shares that goal. A commission on the constitutional roles of the Congress and the President would provide a useful opportunity for both branches to work together toward that common objective.

— The White House, October 24, 1973.

Note: *On November 7, 1973, the House of Representatives and the Senate voted to override the President's veto. As enacted, H.J. Res. 542 is Public Law 93-148 (87 Stat. 555), which became law without the President's signature on November 7.*

4

MILITARY INTERVENTION: HISTORY AND OVERVIEW

EXCLUSIVE WAR POWERS REST WITH THE CONGRESS

Nicholas deB Katzenbach

Nicholas deB Katzenbach is a former Attorney General of the United States. He made the following statement about the constitutional War Powers of the United States Congress before the United States Senate Judiciary Committee.

Points to Consider:

1. According to the Constitution, why does the Congress have exclusive power to make war?

2. Why does the author emphasize the importance and need for Presidential leadership in foreign affairs?

3. What effect has foreign policy had on the average United States citizen?

4. According to the author, how and why should the President involve Congress in momentous decisions?

Excerpted from congressional testimony by Nicholas deB Katzenbach, January 8, 1991.

The Founding Fathers were right when they provided for Congress alone to have the power to declare war.

The Constitution is quite clear that it is Congress who has the exclusive power to declare war. Admittedly, two centuries of somewhat equivocal practice, coupled with expansive Presidential claims under his foreign affairs and Commander in Chief powers, has made it a more difficult legal issue than I think it really is.

One can quibble with the word "war" and point to scores of instances of the use of military force never sanctioned formally by Congress, but unless the grant of Section 8 is to be read out of the Constitution entirely, it applies to any massive use of the military. In those situations where the President has time to seek congressional authorization in advance, he should do so; where not, as in the case of the surprise Japanese attack on Pearl Harbor, he should do so promptly thereafter.

HISTORY

Both Korea and Vietnam, which surely fit anyone's definition of war, confirm this conclusion. In Korea, the President believed that the U.N. Treaty had authorized him in advance to use force in conformity with U.N. sanctions. With respect to Vietnam, the Congress, through the very broad authorization of the Tonkin Gulf resolution, had in fact provided President Johnson with the functional equivalent of a declaration of war.

While I do not agree with President Truman's theory that a treaty can, in essence, amend the Constitution, it was a position held in good faith which, since the enactment of the War Powers Act over a presidential veto, can no longer be maintained today. Whatever else that act did or failed to do, at least it put to rest arguments about that delegation of authority.

Throughout our history, the President has taken the lead in both the formulation and execution of our foreign policy, and I seriously doubt there is any substitute for Presidential leadership. Indeed, the Constitution itself recognizes this fact in the powers it gives the President to speak for the Nation to others.

Similarly, in making the President Commander in Chief of the Armed Forces, the Founding Fathers reflected the dangers of command by committee so apparent in the conduct of the revolution

25

itself. But at the same time, they reserved exclusively to the Congress the power to declare war, and did so in the belief that war was too important a decision to entrust to the judgment of a single person. Why is that not equally so today?

PRESIDENTIAL POWER

To the extent there is doubt as to when or even whether that power comes into effect, it seems to me it stems from the fact that aspects of foreign policy, where Presidential leadership is both clear and necessary, also may involve the use of force. Most of the time, this may amount to no more than showing the flag or landing a few Marines to protect American citizens or property in situations where little possibility of expansion into full-scale hostilities exists—what, in the 19th century parlance was called acts short of war, or, of course, what the Constitution clearly contemplated, self defense. Use of limited force for limited periods of time in support of a known foreign policy has often taken place, without any felt need on the part of either Congress or the President for explicit congressional authorization.

To emphasize the importance and need for Presidential leadership in foreign affairs is to recognize realities, not to denigrate the

---

CONGRESSIONAL WAR POWERS

The framers of the Constitution well knew that giving Congress power over the decision to make war would produce messy debates. But they feared the danger of leaving so grave a decision to one person. As in other aspects of the Constitution, they thought efficiency was less important than safety.

Excerpted from an editorial by Anthony Lewis in the **New York Times**, September 14, 1994.

---

role of Congress. In this century, at least the President needs the support of Congress and of the public for our foreign policy to succeed, and if, despite his considerable power and his advantage, he cannot achieve it, then he must trim his objectives to those which will be supported.

I have no doubt that this basic fact of democracy has restrained and inhibited Presidents from acting in circumstances where later judgment would have supported the wisdom of their having done so. The experience of President Roosevelt between the 1937 quarantine speech and the 1940 election was a classic and bitter example to a generation then forming its views. Indeed, this unhappy restraint may itself have been a factor in the subsequent assertion by Presidents of both parties of extremely broad Presidential prerogatives.

RECENT HISTORY

In recent history, the effect of foreign policy on the average citizen, in terms of both human and monetary costs, has been very great. Given two World Wars, this is hardly surprising, and the Vietnam experience greatly enhanced those feelings of anxiety. Concern for large costs in human lives, in dollars, or risk of massive future involvement for unknown or not understood reasons are powerful sources for public motivation which are bound to be major determinants of foreign policy in a democratic society.

To a President thoroughly committed to the importance and rightness of a particular course of action, the need for Congress and the public to understand and support his policy always runs the risk that, despite his best efforts, they may not. Worse yet,

27

they may disagree. Delay, dissent, debate easily frustrate that policy, damage our national security as he perceives it, severely undercut him with his allies and limit his capacity to lead, and even result in higher costs in lives and money in the future.

All of that, of course, is at bottom fundamental to the functioning of a democracy. However difficult and complex our foreign policy may be, there is no license to free it from the mandates of the Constitution or the constraints of public opinion and the political process, any more than any other difficult and complex problem can be freed from the same constraints. Perhaps the fundamental policy considerations are best perceived in the light that history urged by proponents of Presidential authority. The instances they cite as precedent do not involve matters of political controversy or major commitments of military power. Perhaps some might have debated Panama, for instance, but in each instance the President had sanction to act from Congress and was able to act in a very limited and rapid way.

But if we are talking about a long-term commitment to military engagement, a major military engagement of even short-term duration, or if the consequences of that engagement involve long-term foreign policy goals not previously accepted, the President needs the Congress and the people to both understand and approve his objectives, and, in my opinion, the Congress so requires.

WHAT IS EDITORIAL BIAS?

This activity may be used as an individualized study guide for students in libraries and resource centers or as a discussion catalyst in small group and classroom discussions.

The capacity to recognize an author's point of view is an essential reading skill. The skill to read with insight and understanding involves the ability to detect different kinds of opinions or bias. **Sex bias, race bias, ethnocentric bias, political bias,** and **religious bias** are five basic kinds of opinions expressed in editorials and all literature that attempts to persuade. They are briefly defined below.

FIVE KINDS OF EDITORIAL OPINION OR BIAS

Sex Bias–*The expression of dislike for and/or feeling of superiority over the opposite sex or a particular sexual minority*

Race Bias–*The expression of dislike for and/or feeling of superiority over a racial group*

Ethnocentric Bias–*The expression of a belief that one's own group, race, religion, culture, or nation is superior. Ethnocentric persons judge others by their own standards and values.*

Political Bias–*The expression of political opinions and attitudes about domestic or foreign affairs*

Religious Bias–*The expression of a religious belief or attitude*

29

Guidelines

_____ 1. From the readings in Chapter One, locate five sentences that provide examples of **editorial opinion** or **bias**.

_____ 2. Write down each of the above sentences and determine what kind of bias each sentence represents. Is it **sex bias, race bias, ethnocentric bias, political bias** or **religious bias?**

_____ 3. Make up one-sentence statements that would be an example of each of the following: **sex bias, race bias, ethnocentric bias, political bias** and **religious bias.**

_____ 4. See if you can locate five sentences that are **factual** statements from the readings in Chapter One.

CHAPTER 2

DEMOCRACY AND HUMAN RIGHTS

5 DEMOCRACY AND HUMAN RIGHTS

PROMOTING FREEDOM
AND HUMAN RIGHTS

Larry Diamond

Larry Diamond is a Senior Research Fellow at the Hoover Institution, Stanford University.

Points to Consider:

1. List and explain three key challenges for the United States if it is to be effective in promoting democracy and human rights.

2. Explain the five principles that should determine when to intervene with force.

3. What two steps are vitally important for responding to outrages such as ethnic conflict, aggression and genocide as an international community?

4. What is the most imperative global strategy for American foreign policy in the coming years?

Excerpted from Congressional testimony by Larry Diamond before the House Committee on Foreign Affairs, January and March, 1994.

Because intervention is not possible everywhere does not mean that it should not be undertaken anywhere.

In short, what is distinctive about this moment in history is not simply that the Cold War has ended but that democracy has greater legitimacy and potential in the world than ever before. The word I wish to emphasize, however, is *potential.* The democratic trend remains a very fragile one, and there are growing signs that it may be reaching the point of exhaustion and reversal. A number of civilian, constitutional regimes are functioning in practice so poorly and so undemocratically that Freedom House no longer rates them as "free." In the past few years, this democratic erosion has afflicted countries of real importance to the United States: India, Pakistan, the Philippines, and in our own hemisphere, Nicaragua, Colombia, Venezuela, and Peru. Two countries of vital strategic importance to the United States, Russia and Mexico, have not yet completed the transition to democracy. Indeed, Russia is perched on the precipice of a disastrous political reversal, and there is reason to doubt Mexico's commitment to serious democratic reform.

THE KEY CHALLENGES

There are three types of key challenges for the United States in the coming years if it is to be effective in promoting democracy and human rights. One relates to international structures and institutions in this extremely fluid, post-Cold War world. A second involves structures and institutions within our own country. And the third encompasses the countries that loom as the highest priorities for U.S. foreign policy and democracy assistance efforts in the years ahead.

GLOBAL INSTITUTIONS

The end of the Cold War has left a fluid, volatile, and multipolar world of great instability. For all of its dangers and costs, the Cold War did impose some structure and constraints around a number of potential conflicts. With the demise of these bipolar alliance systems and of communism as an ideology, the world is witnessing a resurgence of ethnic and religious mobilization and, in a number of places, a rapid descent into anarchy. In the years to come we can expect a highly turbulent world in which regimes, boundaries, identities and resources will be intensely and often violently contested. As a global strategy, there is no higher imperative for American foreign policy in the coming years than to contain this spreading turbulence within a new framework of collective security.

Surely, we must begin with realism. More than twenty countries (by some counts, twice that number) are experiencing some form of violent civil conflict. It is well beyond the proper role and available resources of the international community—not to mention the United States alone—to mediate or intervene forcibly in all of these conflicts. However, because intervention is not possible everywhere does not mean that it should not be undertaken anywhere. We must establish a set of principles for when and how to intervene on behalf of political order and human rights. And we must develop, on an urgent basis, the institutions and resources to implement such intervention effectively on a collective, international basis.

INTERVENTION

Five principles should guide the decision of the international community on when and where to intervene with force: 1) the strategic importance of the conflict in threatening regional and international security and vital interests of the democracies; 2) the degree to which the situation violates moral principles and international laws; 3) the potential for the conflict to spill over and spread, either regionally or symbolically and ideologically to other countries; 4) the failure or utter implausibility of non-coercive (e.g., diplomatic and economic) means; and 5) the potential for success with the resources and cooperation that conceivably could be mobilized. In addition, the U.S. must weigh, in pondering whether to seek and mobilize collective intervention, the threat to our own strategic interests. As with the unilateral deployment of American power, so U.N. and other collective security forces should never be committed unless they are deployed on a sufficient scale, with the authority, firepower, and logistical support to perform their mission effectively. A major lesson of the recent debacle of U.N.-mediated elections in Angola, and of the problems we are having in Somalia, Yugoslavia, and Cambodia, is that peacekeeping cannot be done on the cheap.

I stress this issue first because international aggression, state violence against minority groups, separatist terrorism, and violent conflict between different ethnic, regional, and religious groups

Reprinted by permission: **Tribune Media Services.**

are likely to represent the greatest threats to human rights and democracy in the years ahead. Unless we establish a framework for responding to these outrages as an international community under law, the effort to expand and strengthen democracy will, in many parts of the world, drown in a sea of blood. We must bear in mind that it is not only the afflicted countries that are affected. As we are seeing in Eastern Europe, a major civil war between nationality groups inevitably has regional consequences and reverberations. Unchecked, such conflict could destabilize neighboring democracies and give a green light to ultranationalists and ethnic chauvinists throughout a region.

THE CHALLENGE

Two steps are vitally important for meeting this challenge. **First**, we must completely overhaul and strengthen the peacekeeping and peacemaking capacities of the United Nations. Future U.N. security missions must be prepared not only to stand and observe but to fight actively to make and enforce peace. Warring parties that clearly reject the U.N.-mediated peace process and seek monopoly power by force—such as the Khmer Rouge, the Serbian armies, UNITA in Angola, and quite possibly the competing warlords in Somalia—must be isolated internationally and confronted militarily. The mission of U.N. peacemaking forces must be clearly articulated and authorized by the Security Council. It will require—if the civilized world is serious about collective security—much greater commitments of troops and weapons and fundamental changes in operational structure to provide much more effective command and control.

Second, we must strengthen the United Nations itself as an institution capable of resolving conflict and promoting democracy and human rights. This, too, requires major institutional reforms, combatting corruption, pruning rampant waste and overstaffing, improving performance criteria and evaluation, and enhancing the authority of the United Nations Security Council by giving permanent membership to Germany and Japan. Many good reform ideas have recently been advanced, including the creation of a vigorous and autonomous inspector general within the U.N. Unless we tackle soon the hard organizational issues, the U.N. simply will not have the legitimacy and capacity to meet the urgent challenges ahead.

Promoting democracy abroad must be a global effort. If we conceive of democracy as a continuous phenomenon, rather than something that is merely "present" or "absent," then there is some possibility for democratic progress virtually everywhere in the world, and no country should be written off. The most important requirement for rapid democratic progress is not a high level of wealth but a commitment on the part of a country's elite, and among key groups in civil society, to make democracy work. Where we find that, even in poor and peripheral countries such as Nepal, we should support it with more political assistance and foreign aid.

In strategic terms, however, it remains true that some countries are more important than others, both to our own immediate national security and to the emerging shape of the "new world order."

CONCLUSION

Advancing the cause of democracy in the world will be a formidable challenge in the coming years. In the midst of spreading conflict and instability, it will not be easy to maintain the democracies that have recently come into being, and it will be harder still to increase their number. The keys to progress will be patience, steadfastness, institutional innovation, and increasing cooperation on the part of the established democracies around the

> # HISTORY'S LESSON
>
> History's lesson is clear: When a war-weary America with-
> drew from the international stage following World War I, the
> world spawned militarism, fascism, and aggression
> unchecked, plunging mankind into another devastating con-
> flict.
>
> President George Bush, "America—The Last Best Hope for Man on Earth,"
> **Vital Speeches of the Day**, January 15, 1993.

world. The United States must lead, but our democratic allies—
Europe, Japan, Canada, Australia, and others—must also commit
their resources and prestige to the protection and expansion of
democracy and human rights. And increasingly, we will need to
work through the United Nations and regional bodies to promote
democracy and collective security. Promoting democracy cannot
be our only foreign policy goal, but neither can it be effective as a
partial and piecemeal strategy. The Cold War is over, but we
remain the only country that can catalyze the world to move in
new directions. Now more than ever, we must continue to think
and act globally.

6   DEMOCRACY AND HUMAN RIGHTS

WHY U.S.-BACKED GOVERNMENTS MURDER CHURCH WORKERS

Jack Nelson-Pallmeyer

Jack Nelson-Pallmeyer lived and worked in Central America for several years, and is still a frequent traveler to the region. He is the author of War Against the Poor: Low-Intensity Conflict and Christian Faith *(Orbis Books).*

Points to Consider:

1. Explain why the United States government is at war against liberation theology and churches that seek to empower the poor.

2. Describe the five unpardonable sins committed by Third World governments or social change movements.

3. What is the meaning of low-intensity conflict?

4. How does low-intensity conflict make warfare less visible to U.S. people?

5. Why has the spirit of the poor continued its resistance?

Jack Nelson-Pallmeyer, "Why U.S.-Backed Governments Murder Church Workers," **Sojourners**, December 1990. Reprinted with permission from **Sojourners**, 2401 15th St. NM, Washington, D.C. 20009, (202) 328-8842.

The experience of Christian lay leader "Ramon" in El Salvador is typical. In order to discourage Ramon's religious activities, the Salvadoran military took his son, peeled off his skin, cut off his testicles, and hung his body on a cross.

On November 16, 1989, the world was stunned by the murder in El Salvador of six Jesuit priests, their housekeeper, and her daughter. Americas Watch testified to Congress that the Jesuits were murdered by members of a U.S.-trained elite unit (the Atlacatl Battalion) with a long history of human rights violations.

Missing from most discussions of who ultimately is to blame for the Jesuit murders is acknowledgment that the U.S. government is actively and consciously targeting progressive church workers as enemies. As part of its broader strategy of warfare against the poor called "low-intensity conflict," our government is at war against liberation theology and against churches that seek to empower the poor. Whether or not agents of the U.S. government ordered the massacre of the Jesuits, the United States is morally and practically responsible for their deaths and those of numerous religious workers.

THIRD WORLD NATIONS

There are five unpardonable sins committed by Third World governments or social change movements: reclaiming a sense of national dignity, exercising political power outside the control of economic elites, redistributing wealth from the rich to the poor, building alliances with progressive churches around common agendas to empower the poor, and developing a military independent of U.S. control.

The United States is determined to punish those guilty of one or more of these sins by using a flexible array of weapons within its low-intensity conflict arsenal. If Christians are complicit in such sins by challenging political and economic injustices or by forming alliances with groups that share similar goals, they, too, will be targets of U.S. warfare.

The basic problem confronting the United States in Third World settings is maintaining the disparity between its wealth and the poverty of others on whom its wealth depends. George Kennan, as head of the State Department's planning staff, stated in 1948:

39

"We have about 50 percent of the world's wealth, but only 6.3 percent of its populations...Our real task in the coming period is to devise a pattern of relationships which will permit us to maintain this position of disparity."

U.S. STRATEGY

U.S. strategists see vital U.S. interests under attack throughout the so-called Third World. "As the leading 'have' power," U.S. Gen. Maxwell Taylor stated, "we may expect to have to fight to protect our national valuables against envious 'have nots.'" In other words, the poor must remain poor and limit their consumption if we are to continue our pattern of wasteful consumption.

U.S. low-intensity conflict strategy is designed to preserve the disparity between the affluent or opulent few and the impoverished majority. Such disparity gives rise to social turmoil in many Third World countries, and the church is not insulated from such turmoil. U.S. policies reward or punish Christians and churches depending on whether they help maintain or challenge this disparity. For example, conservative Catholic leaders such as Cardinal Obando y Bravo in Nicaragua, right-wing fundamentalist sects, and TV evangelists such as Jimmy Swaggart and Pat Robertson receive direct and indirect support from the U.S. government.

PERSECUTION

One major form of indirect support is that they are not persecuted by U.S.-backed governments. This helps explain the success of their evangelization efforts. People consciously or unconsciously learn that confining one's faith to the realm of personal piety is much safer than a faith that leads one to confront unjust social structures.

Other segments of the Catholic and Protestant churches experience constant persecution at the hands of U.S.-backed governments. Repression is targeted against Christian groups that have undergone a fundamental transformation of faith in light of the life experience of the poor.

A "colonial theology" that justifies economic exploitation by admonishing the poor to obey authority, accept poverty as God's will, and wait patiently for a heavenly reward is challenged by a liberating theology that stresses the dignity of the human person,

Reprinted with permission from **Star Tribune,** Minneapolis.

poverty as an offense against God and humanity, the sinfulness of unjust social structures, God's promise of liberation to the poor, and the example of Jesus in living out faith to its ultimate consequence.

LIBERATION THEOLOGY

The U.S. war against liberation theology and progressive Christians is part of its broader war against the organized poor who are seeking to restructure the unjust societies in which they are living...

Countering liberation theology often means a brutal war of intimidation against Christians involved in working with the poor. The experience of a Christian lay leader "Ramon," in El Salvador, is typical. In order to discourage Ramon's religious activities, the Salvadoran military took his son, peeled off his skin, cut off his testicles, and hung his body on a cross. "Our crime," Ramon told me, "is to be poor and ask for bread...without land we cannot plant. There is no work...And so we demonstrate. But to speak of justice is to be called a communist, to ask for bread is subversive."

The war against progressive Christians and churches is a strategic priority for the U.S. military and its allies. Secret documents leaked from a 1987 meeting of the Conference of American

Armies places the persecution of the churches in context. Signed by military commanders from Argentina, Uruguay, Chile, Paraguay, Bolivia, Brazil, Peru, Ecuador, Colombia, Venezuela, Panama, Honduras, Guatemala, El Salvador, and the United States, the documents portray liberation theology as a fundamental enemy that must be countered through continental security measures that include the coordination of military intelligence and operations.

LOW-INTENSITY CONFLICT

The United States is confronting a series of low-intensity conflicts—conflicts that are low-intensity relative to the violence traditionally associated with nuclear or conventional wars—throughout the Third World. Low-intensity conflict also refers to the strategy by which the United States defends its "vital" interests. The persecution of progressive churches is part of this strategy.

It is an Orwellian term. The murder of Salvadoran Archbishop Oscar Romero, the blood of the Jesuit priests, the deaths of more than 70,000 Salvadorans over the past 10 years, and the destruction of neighboring Nicaragua remind us that low-intensity conflict causes high-intensity pain.

Low-intensity conflict strategy isn't new, but it has undergone significant revisions. After the Vietnam War ripped apart the nation and caused serious divisions within the military, strategists set out to improve the capability of the United States to intervene in Third World settings. What emerged was a totalitarian-like strategy that integrates economic, psychological, diplomatic, and military aspects of warfare into a comprehensive whole.

Recent interventions have sought to control hearts and minds, not simply hold or win territory. This increases the importance of psychological warfare, including managing terror against civilians, using fundamentalist sects to reinforce conservative ideologies, and targeting repression against progressive churches...Vietnam demonstrated the limits of acceptable carnage. The U.S. people grew weary of a bloody war...

Low-intensity conflict strategy makes warfare less visible to the people in the United States. U.S. strategists fear our basic decency even as they count on and cultivate our racism. They believe, perhaps with good reason, that we will remain indifferent to most atrocities as long as other non-U.S. and usually non-white soldiers

> ## KILLERS IN U.S. HELICOPTERS
>
> When the Salvadoran National Guard came to her village in United States-supplied helicopters, they chopped all the children to bits and threw them to the village pigs. "The soldiers laughed all the while," Luisa told me. "What were they trying to kill?" she asked, crying.
>
> We went around the circle. Each woman told her story. The same story. Each had had nothing. They had worked, generations of them, all day, every day on someone else's land. Their children were parasite-ridden or starving. Visits to the landowners, the patrons, eventually had brought in the Guard. "We asked for food. They gave us bullets."
>
> All of the women still had tears to cry as they told of brothers, husbands gathered into a circle and set on fire after their legs had been broken. They told of trees heavy with women hanging by the wrists, a sister or a godmother among them, all with breasts cut off and facial skin peeled back, all slowly bleeding to death. A frenzy went with each telling, as though the women had yet to find a place inside themselves to contain it.
>
> Elizabeth Hanly, "Refugee Women and Children," **Christianity and Crisis**, December 10, 1984, p. 467.

and citizens do the dying in defense of U.S. privileges.

There is no politically costly draft, no direct new taxes to fund a foreign war, and few U.S. soldiers returning in body bags. The emphasis is on quick-strike forces, uses of surrogate troops such as the Nicaraguan contras or the Salvadoran military, and on covert actions of which the Iran-contra affair was merely the tip of the iceberg...

DECISIVE ACTION

Not all conflicts can be addressed within the framework of low-intensity warfare strategy. The massive U.S. military response to the crisis in the Gulf illustrates that when strategic resources such as oil are at stake, the United States will act decisively. More important, some U.S. military leaders have been slow to embrace low-intensity conflict strategy because of their fear of losing power and influence. Low-intensity conflicts, they fear, will not in themselves provide justification for huge military expenditures. The U.S. military response to Iraq's takeover of Kuwait was fueled more by the military-industrial complex's fear of a "peace dividend" in light of changing U.S.-Soviet relations than by any other factor.

However, low-intensity-conflict advocates have much to celebrate. The electoral victory of Violeta Chamorro in Nicaragua's election proved the viability of a policy that caused more than $17 billion in damage to a country of three million people...More broadly, the war against the poor is gathering momentum. Defending "our national valuables" in Third World settings has taken on increased significance in light of U.S. economic decline relative to Western Europe and Japan...

THE SPIRIT

In a more positive light, the spirit of resistance continues. Many progressive church workers have returned to El Salvador and resumed their work among the poor. In Nicaragua, there is strong organized resistance to dismantling revolutionary gains in land tenure, education, and health care. At home, pressure to end aid to El Salvador continues to build, and a religious fast at Fort Benning, Georgia, has raised awareness of ongoing training of Salvadoran military forces on U.S. soil.

In a recent issue of *Sojourners*, Jon Sobrino reminded us that "you cannot be a believer in God today in this world if...growing oppression and poverty is not your central issue." Churches are being persecuted and popular movements are under attack as a matter of U.S. "low-intensity conflict" strategy. Ultimately, what is at stake for us is the essence and integrity of our faith and our claim to be human beings.

7 DEMOCRACY AND HUMAN RIGHTS

EXPORTING DEMOCRACY

Bette Bao Lord

Bette Bao Lord is the Chairperson of Freedom House. Her testimony was heard before the House Committee on Foreign Affairs on "United States Policy Regarding Human Rights and Democracy."

Points to Consider:

1. What is the primary challenge for the American people, regarding the break up of the Soviet Union and the fall of Communism in Eastern Europe?

2. Why are democracies still the most successful model for nurturing a vibrant society?

3. According to Freedom House, has democracy triumphed in a convincing fashion?

4. What must the United States do for human rights and democratization to have ethical and moral importance in the world?

Excerpted from testimony by Bette Bao Lord before the House Committee on Foreign Affairs, March 10, 1993.

Concern for human rights and democracy is intrinsic to our integrity.

The breakup of the Soviet Union and the fall of Communism in Eastern Europe present many challenges to promoting human rights and democracy. Our commitment to these vital elements of our foreign policy, however, must go beyond those countries directly affected by the end of the Cold War. For meaningful progress and peace, our vision must be sustained by the excellence of our own example and must be global in scope.

THE CHALLENGE

The primary challenge is for the American people to appreciate that, in an increasingly shrinking and interdependent world, foreign policy is, in fact, a key domestic issue. It affects U.S. jobs, commerce, the environment, public health and national security. In a global economy and a technological age, neo-isolationism and disengagement from world affairs are precisely the wrong prescriptions at the wrong time. Our critical task is to counter public indifference by articulating a clear and cogent policy based on democratic values, human rights, justice and opportunity.

Freedom House believes democracy-building and human rights reinforce each other. But sadly some democratically-elected governments are indeed undemocratic. We must hold all governments accountable, linking assistance and cooperation with implementing universally accepted standards.

We offer, not foist, our system on others.

DEMOCRACY AND HUMAN RIGHTS

In the final analysis, democracies are still the most successful model for nurturing a vibrant society, responsive government, a free press, effective unions, domestic harmony and global cooperation. America is a microcosm of the world. And our reliance on and respect for the individual is the basis of our civil society.

For human rights and democratization to have ethical and moral weight, our concerns in the post-Cold War world must go beyond the usual areas of attention to include a greater emphasis on Africa and Asia. Since the Soviet sphere is no more, anti-Communism has lost its legitimacy as a refuge for scoundrels and human rights abusers. Thus we can broaden our efforts to make

46

Cartoon by Jim Morin.

the world a smaller, better and safer place.

Universal principles need to be universally applied to have meaning. With a single standard for all, we can avoid the moral pitfalls that once compromised our human rights policy. The next few years are critical. Discredited tenets of Communism must not be replaced by other retrogressive isms.

With Communism's demise in the USSR and the Eastern Bloc and the disintegration of the Warsaw Pact, age-old ethnic animosities make democratic transitions even more difficult. Economic dislocation tempts backlash. Ultra-nationalists, former Communists and other reactionary forces tap discontent to undermine change.

GLOBAL SECURITY

The absence of an effective collective security apparatus and the presence of minorities straddling borders have led to regional instability. The horrific war in former Yugoslavia and the brushfire conflicts in Georgia, Azerbaijan, Moldova and even Russia may preview broader conflagration in the former Soviet empire.

We must not allow fear of spreading fundamentalism to divert our attention from continued and egregious violations of political, civil and human rights in Arab kingdoms and sheikdoms.

47

Also nationalism, given its historic and cultural roots, is difficult to address. Thus an aggressive, long-term plan for economic renewal must accompany building democratic infrastructure and institutions. Sharing fairly in economic gains will lessen everyone's stake in strife.

The end of ideological struggle has changed the geopolitical equation. Regimes and states once propped up by massive Soviet or East bloc aid are today either completely isolated (Cuba and North Korea) or, in the case of several West African countries (Benin, Gabon) they are looking to the West for assistance by moving toward democratic and free-market reforms.

Some authoritarian regimes once backed by the United States to counter the expansion of Soviet influence (South Africa, El Salvador) are heeding domestic and international pressures to liberalize. They need to be watched. Others (Angola, Haiti), however, have responded with renewed violence.

While nascent democracies struggle with the profoundly difficult and protracted task of reshaping politics conducive to pluralism, many existing democracies are divided by ethnic-religious tensions (India) or domestic violence, widescale corruption and narco-terrorism (Colombia and Peru). Democracy's recent toehold may be slipping.

ASIAN NATIONS

China persists in repression. The situation in Tibet remains despicable. Vietnam and Laos, like China, have yet to couple economic liberalization with political liberalization. Both are indispensable to true progress. Burma's illegitimate government continues to oppress its citizenry. Indonesia continues to violate human rights in East Timor.

In the emerging Central Asian states, vestiges of Stalinism as well as historic, anti-democratic factors impede progress in Tajikistan, Uzbekistan and Turkmenistan. Ethnic and religious rivalries could intensify and convert to intra-state conflicts. Muslim fundamentalism has emerged as a potent threat in Egypt, Algeria and elsewhere in North Africa and the Middle East.

Finally, there are ongoing conflicts in Angola, Somalia, Sudan, Liberia, Afghanistan, Azerbaijan, Armenia, Cambodia, Burma and the Balkans. Statecraft in the post-Communist world must entail a

> # POLITICAL ISOLATION
>
> Experience shows that political protectionism—isolation-ism—is no more valid than trade protectionism. Experience also shows that a delayed response, as in Rwanda, runs up the cost in lives and money. Both lessons applied in the '30s, which brought World War II, and both apply now.
>
> Robert J. White, "Old Lessons Apply: Ignore Crises Now, Pay the Price Later," **Star Tribune**, August 11, 1994, p. 25A.

multilateral approach forged by consensus and international cooperation whenever possible. The U.S. must clearly use its power and moral leadership to spearhead peacekeeping and humanitarian efforts around the world. Unilateral intervention should be resisted. U.S. policy must be a mix of advocacy and action.

Freedom House is heartened by President Clinton's endorsement of several programs to expand and export democracy. At the same time, some disparities between campaign promises and policy must be clarified.

While blame for the deteriorating situation in Bosnia must be laid, above all, squarely on the cowardly failure of the Europeans to respond, the Bush administration shares responsibility. Current Balkan policy should be strengthened. Serbian aggression must not be rewarded. Perpetrators of war crimes and genocide must be punished.

As a human rights organization, we hope the new Administration will focus the same attention on foreign policy concerns as it does on domestic issues. Washington must show leadership. It must articulate an active, multifaceted and comprehensive foreign policy in a world no longer defined or constrained by outmoded ideologies. The rules have changed. The world today may in fact be more intractable than at any time in the last few decades. Fundamentalism, xenophobia, zealotry and fear, particularly in nuclear nations, pose a clear danger to their citizens, neighbors, and the world. Nuclear non-proliferation, disarmament and related issues may be as critical in the future as in the past.

CURRENT POLICY

Rather than focus on what is wrong about a still-developing U.S. policy, I would rather look at the opportunities, amplified by new technologies, for progress. Today the United States is the only superpower. To be worthy of that stature, America must frame and implement human rights and democratization as an integral part of its broader foreign policy. To be effective, America must be engaged, disciplined, steadfast and consistent.

If Freedom House's assessment of the challenges to our foreign policy seems broadly drawn, it is meant to be. Other countries may adopt a narrower, more parochial concept of national interest or a more pragmatic view of their role in the world. But not America. Concern for human rights and democracy is intrinsic to our integrity.

America has committed itself to democratization and economic assistance to the former Soviet Union and Eastern Europe. But their importance to our national interests is not reflected in our approach to date. We must expand our investment. After World War II, the U.S. provided massive aid to rebuild the economies vitiated by years of destruction. The dividend, along with prosperity, was German and Japanese stability. While economic constraints at home prevent us from implementing another Marshall Plan, we can offer more.

America spent tens of trillions of dollars and tens of thousands of lives promoting freedom and democracy during the Cold War. We have come too far and paid too dearly to shirk our responsibilities. The cost of assisting the former USSR and Eastern Europe is small change to the cost should democracy fail there. Hardline, nationalist depotism threatens much of the region largely because national and regional economics remain in shambles.

Therefore, large financial institutions must be persuaded to become more engaged. The International Monetary Fund (IMF) and the World Bank must take the big political picture into account in deliberating on loans to the former Soviet Union.

We must convince the American people that there can be no "peace dividend" if chaos reigns abroad.

8   DEMOCRACY AND HUMAN RIGHTS

EMPIRE AS A WAY OF LIFE

William Appleman Williams

William Appleman Williams, now deceased, taught in the history department at Oregon State University. He was president of the Organization of American Historians, and this article is adapted from his book, Empire as a Way of Life.

Points to Consider:

1. How is the term *empire* defined?

2. What relationship did early American leaders have with imperial ideas?

3. What does the author mean by the term "imperial farmers"? How did President Lincoln relate ideas of imperialism to American farmers?

4. What is the real meaning of the National Security Council Document No. 68, approved by Harry Truman in 1950?

5. What was President Eisenhower's attitude toward an American empire?

William Appleman Williams, *Empire as a Way of Life*, **The Nation**, August 2-9, 1980. This article is reprinted from **The Nation** magazine. (©1980) The Nation Company, L.P.

Let us start with a workable definition of empire: the use and abuse, and the ignoring, of other people for one's own welfare and convenience. Now in truth, America was born and bred of empire. That does not mean that we are unique; indeed, just the opposite. We are part and parcel of the imperial outreach of Western Europe that came to dominate the world. But therein lies the irreducible cause of our present predicament. We have from the beginning defined and viewed ourselves as unique. The differences between ourselves and other nations are not incidental but they are irrelevant to the fundamental issue. We are different only because we acquired the empire at a very low cost, because the rewards have been enormous and because until now we have masked our imperial truth with the rhetoric of freedom.

THE CHINESE

But we do have a bench mark. Once upon a time, about a century before America was rediscovered by Christopher Columbus, at least the fifth time someone had done it, the Chinese sent seven massive fleets westward to Africa and perhaps on into the Atlantic Ocean. The ships measured between 400 and 500 feet, and there were enough of them to carry upward of 37,000 people. Their so-called junks were impressive intercontinental missiles. The Chinese came, they traded, they observed. They made no effort to create an empire or even an imperial sphere of influence. Upon returning home, their reports engendered a major debate. The decision was made to burn and otherwise destroy the great fleets and concentrate on developing Chinese society and culture.

The point is not to present the Chinese as immaculately disinterested, or whiter than white. It is simply to note that we now know that the capacity for empire does not lead irresistibly or inevitably to the reality of empire. The Chinese, driven south by the Mongols and other invaders, could easily have rationalized empire as necessity. They chose instead to defeat the invaders and develop their own culture in its almost infinite variations on the two themes of Confucianism and Taoism.

Not so with Western Europeans, including our English forefathers. They were not content with exploration and nonviolent intercourse with other cultures. From the beginning, the Western Europeans went for global empire. We Americans were conceived and born and bred of that imperial conception and way of life. We can explain that, even defend it, but we cannot deny it...

Cartoon by Richard Wright.

AMERICAN LEADERS

The American leaders who made the Revolution and the Constitution were familiar with all those imperial ideas. And in Virginia, for example, men of property had realized the value of imperial expansion for controlling the white poor long before Patrick Henry began talking about liberty or death. Indeed, the dialogue between other Virginians provides an excellent insight into the development of an imperial way of life.

James Madison never discounted the importance of economic expansion, commercial or territorial; but he stressed the need for surplus social space to avoid political turmoil when he advanced his famous argument about extending the sphere in defense of the Constitution. In denying the conventional wisdom that a republican government could survive only in a small state, Madison was implicitly arguing that empire is the price of freedom...

For his part, John Taylor of Caroline County, Virginia, was devastating. He began by mocking Madison's euphemism for imperial expansion—"extending the sphere"... Taylor understood that America had embraced an imperial way of life. He knew, Thomas Paine to the contrary notwithstanding, that the United States had not begun the world over again. No wonder he ultimately lost his respect for Thomas Jefferson.

Jefferson was far too intelligent not to understand Taylor.

Indeed, too smart not to recognize the meaning of the Chinese decision that I have described. He alluded to that in one letter and, sensing the implications, quickly dropped the subject. In that respect, and it is an important one, Jefferson was much more like us ordinary folk than either Madison or Taylor. Jefferson wanted to have it every way imaginable. He wanted to be the best hope on earth. He wanted to civilize the heathen. He wanted Canada and Florida and the rest of the continent...

He knew the meaning of anguish about it all, but he went for empire. Half honestly and half dishonestly. The honest part was saying that empire is necessary for freedom and social order as defined by Locke and Bacon. The dishonest part was asserting that empire did not subvert freedom. So between them, Jefferson and Madison used their sixteen years as President to institutionalize empire as a way of life. Taylor went home and gave it all up for lost...

IMPERIAL FARMERS

There is also a fine irony in the way that the great war for American freedom led on to ever more empire. And it is fitting that Lincoln provides us with an insight into the dynamics of that process. He knew, by December 1862, that the gamble on a quick victory had been lost. He had to have money and men in large quantities. He therefore appealed to the imperial tradition. Speaking to the agricultural majority, he wasted no euphemisms. He told them they had to stay the course because it was not enough to have access to the world via New York and San Francisco. It was also necessary to control New Orleans and the Gulf of Mexico...

The significance of Lincoln's appeal to Western farmers to fight on for imperial objectives upsets historians of every political persuasion. Radicals resist the notion that ordinary folk support imperialism. Conservatives cannot easily come to terms with the reality that empire is related to liberty as they define it. And liberals long to resolve the dilemma by defining empire as global freedom and welfare.

Despite that tide of wisdom, I suggest that American farmers of the nineteenth century provide us with a revealing illustration of the dynamic evolution of our imperial way of life. They began by defining empire as ever more free or cheap land and concluded by demanding strong government action to help them penetrate

PHILIPPINE-AMERICAN WAR

Tragically, hundreds of thousands of Filipinos perished in battlefields and in refugee camps. By its own account, the U.S. military estimated that about 600,000 Filipino lives were lost just on Luzon island alone (about one-sixth of the entire population of the island). An additional 200,000 Filipinos were killed in military campaigns on Samar island. In total, nearly a million Filipinos perished during the brief but brutal pacification campaign waged by U.S. troops.

Initially, the U.S. military wrapped press coverage of the war under strict censorship. But letters written by U.S. soldiers reached the press back home; more information on the savage conduct of the war spread in the U.S. Soon, an anti-imperialism movement flourished. Joined by influential intellectuals such as Jane Addams, Mark Twain and William James, the Anti-Imperialist League denounced Washington for its brutal pacification campaigns in the Philippines.

Vito Inoferio, "Panama Intervention Reminds Filipinos of a Tragic Past," **Global Perspectives**, Winter 1990, p. 1-2, 8-9.

and hold foreign markets. All in the name of freedom and security. That process is worth examining closely because it reveals a great deal about our American outlook as it developed in the twentieth century...

THE KOREAN WAR

Nothing documents that as clearly as National Security Council Document No. 68, approved by President Harry S. Truman in April 1950... NSC-68 begins with a disturbing review of how all the old empires have collapsed. It summarized that overview with this revealing conclusion:

"Even if there were no Soviet Union we would face the great problem...[that] the absence of order among nations is becoming less and less tolerable." Then defining the United States as the only nation capable of imposing such order, it makes the Soviet Union the focus of the effort. It candidly admits Churchill's main point: the United States and its allies possess greater power— enough to deter any direct attack.

But, unlike Churchill, American leaders concluded that such power must be further increased and deployed to "foster a fundamental change in the nature of the Soviet system"; "foster the seeds of destruction within the Soviety system," and foment and support "unrest and revolt in selected strategic satellite countries." As for means: "any means, covert or overt, violent or nonviolent." Then, pointing to the experience of World War II, the policy makers confidently predicted that the increase in military spending would prevent the possibility of any socially and politically explosive "real decrease in the standard of living."

In a rare moment of candor, Secretary of State Dean Acheson admitted in 1953 that he and Truman might not have been able to sustain their grandiose imperial policy if the North Koreans had not "come along and saved us"...

On balance, however, it was simply one of those wars that anybody could have counted on to erupt sometime. Both halves of that divided country were dying to go to war to unite themselves. That "old deb'l" nationalism had been raised to fever pitch by very strong shots of mutually exclusive theology. In any event, the debate about who bears ultimate responsibility obscures the fundamental issue of the response by Truman and Acheson.

Clearly, when the Secretary acknowledged that Korea "saved us," he did not mean in the sense of preventing the defeat or the destruction of the United States. He meant only that it allowed the Government to implement the apocalyptic imperial strategy of NSC-68. Primed and ready, armed (or driven) psychologically as well as with the heady rhetoric of that document, they simply went to war. They bypassed the Congress and the public and confronted both with an accomplished fact. A few phone calls, and it was done. Go to bed at peace and wake up at war.

It was even more dramatic than the subsequent intervention in Vietnam as a demonstration of the centralization of power inherent in empire as a way of life. The State had literally been compressed or consolidated into the President and his like-minded appointee...

EMPIRE AT BAY

The empire had been brought to bay. Dwight David Eisenhower understood that essential truth, and further realized that the future character of American society depended upon how the culture responded. His first objective after he became President in 1952 was to end the Korean police action before it spiraled into World War III. That accomplished, he set about to calm Americans, cool them off and refocus their attention and energies on domestic development. He was a far more perceptive and cagey leader than many people realized at the time—or later.

The image of a rather absent-minded, sometimes bumbling if not incoherent, Uncle Ike was largely his own shrewd cover for his serious efforts to get control of the military (and other militant cold warriors), to decrease tension with Russia and somehow begin to deal with the fundamental distortions of American society. He clearly understood that crusading imperial police actions were extremely dangerous, and he was determined to avoid World War III. When Britain, France and Israel attacked Egypt in 1956 over the nationalization of the Suez Canal, the President called British Prime Minister Anthony Eden and scolded him sharply: "Anthony, you must have gone out of your mind."

When the moment came, Eisenhower could be just as blunt with Americans. A good many of them were probably shocked when, in his farewell address of 1961, he spoke candidly and forcefully about the military-industrial complex that since 1939 had become the axis of the American political economy. That was such a catchy phrase that not many of them noticed that he went on to assault the distortion of education involved in that consolidation of power. The historically free and critical university, he noted, "the fountainhead of free ideas and scientific discovery, has experienced a revolution in the conduct of research...A governmental contract becomes virtually a substitute for intellectual curiosity."

The speech was not an aberration: Eisenhower had become ever more deeply concerned with those issues after retiring from the Army. Thus, while it is true that he was not an intellectual, and was conservative in many ways, it is also true that he had a firm sense of how the State had gradually taken over the very process of creating and controlling basic ideas—the ways of making sense of reality. Or, in a different way, how the State used its extensive control of information, and its ability to make major decisions in the name of security, to create an ideology ever more defined in content as well as rhetoric as an imperial way of life...

WHAT ARE THE RIGHT QUESTIONS?

I like to return to the questions raised by our history:

Is the idea and reality of America possible without empire?

Can you even imagine America as not an empire?

The truth of it is that I think they are incompatible.

Do you want to imagine a new America or do you want to pre-serve the empire?

9   DEMOCRACY AND HUMAN RIGHTS

THE MORAL ARGUMENT FOR U.S. LEADERSHIP

Henry R. Nau

Henry R. Nau is a professor at George Washington University and is also the author of The Myth of America's Decline *(Oxford University Press 1992).*

Points to Consider:

1. What is the moral argument for United States leadership?

2. What three new guidelines are suggested for United States foreign policy?

3. How are United States relations with industrial countries portrayed by the author?

4. Describe the role of new technology in foreign relations.

5. How should the United States conduct foreign policy in the post-Cold War world?

Unless the U.S. remains free and progressive for each of its citizens who seeks equality, it loses its moral core and its moral right to use force in world affairs.

Presidents Bush and Clinton have had trouble integrating both power and ideals in post-Cold War foreign policy. Mr. Bush pursued a "new world order" based on resisting territorial aggression and balancing power, but he lacked vision. Mr. Clinton promised a more visionary foreign policy to help build democracy around the world, particularly in Russia, but he is cutting defense outlays by much more than Mr. Bush proposed and seems reluctant to use force in foreign affairs, even to the point of accepting the results of territorial conquest in the former Yugoslavia.

Containment, the policy that guided American foreign policy in the Cold War, succeeded because it *did* integrate American power and ideals. NSC-68, the document that laid out the containment doctrine, premised America's defense not just on power but also on the moral worth of a free society "founded upon the dignity and worth of the individual." It authorized the use of force to defend that society only to the extent that such force was "appropriately calculated" and "not so excessive or misdirected as to make us enemies of the people instead of the evil men who enslaved them."

THE WORLD'S TEST CASE

New guidelines for U.S. foreign policy after the Cold War must also start with a clear sense of America's moral self-worth. Unless the U.S. remains free and progressive for each of its citizens who seeks equality, it loses its moral core and its moral right to use force in world affairs.

America is the democratic world's most diverse society. Nearly 30% of the population belongs to visually distinct racial or ethnic minorities—more than three times the percentage of any other industrial nation. As such, America is the world's continuing test case for a tolerant, multicultural democracy. That it has met this test so far is its greatest asset in foreign affairs. The world tends to trust America's leadership, over that of more homogeneous societies, because America copes daily with ethnic and racial issues within its own society.

Thus President Clinton should not view time spent on foreign policy as a diversion from domestic affairs or portray domestic pri-

Cartoon by Dale Stephanos.

orities as being in conflict with foreign responsibilities. Anything he accomplishes domestically contributes directly to foreign policy. Similarly, if he ignores offenses to freedom and human rights abroad, it will not be long before such cynicism erodes tolerant multicultural relations at home.

A second guideline for the new foreign policy follows from the first. American interests are inextricably tied up with those of other democratic societies. Containment recognized this fact in the common institutions—NATO, GATT, etc.—that powered the Western nations to victory in the Cold War.

INDUSTRIAL NATIONS

Today, for the first time, all of the industrial nations are solidly democratic. U.S. relations with these countries have transcended traditional balance-of-power politics. Democratic states—defined in terms of a broad voting franchise, fair and competitive elections, and protection of basic individual rights—have never fought one another. They do not even escalate disputes to the level of military threats but resolve disputes through open procedures of law, diplomacy and commerce.

That does not mean that industrial nations do not compete economically and culturally. But to fail to distinguish rival economies or rival capitalisms from the rival nationalisms and other "isms" that have divided industrial states over the past two centuries is merchant parochialism at its worst. President Clinton would do well not to let his fundamental policies toward Japan or Europe be decided exclusively by trade negotiators.

Instead, relations among industrial nations should be guided by a third principle of post-Cold War foreign policy: the need and opportunity to build democracies and free markets in the former communist countries and parts of the developing world. Because democracies do not fight one another, this policy is not idealism but a realistic investment in national security.

In this national security context, trade policies are not just about jobs. They are about creating an atmosphere of openness and freedom that enables reforming countries to find their own way peacefully toward greater prosperity and pluralism. If the old democracies fragment over trade issues, the new democracies will surely fail.

Moreover, open markets do not cost jobs. They create and change jobs. Employment in the U.S. grew by 20 million jobs over the past 20 years, 50% more than in any other industrial nation. This overall job creation represented a shift from lower- to higher-skilled manufacturing and service industries, with higher wages for the skilled and no net loss of manufacturing output as a share of gross national product. This shift was induced not by imports, but by technology.

NEW TECHNOLOGY

Because America has been more willing than Europe or even Japan to put new technology to work in both manufacturing and service industries, America had higher productivity growth in manufacturing in the 1980s than all other industrial countries with the exception of Britain and Japan (although the U.S. had caught up with both of these countries by the end of the decade) and is more competitive today by far in the service sectors (telecommunications, finance, airlines, etc.) than any of its industrial allies.

U.S. manufacturing exports, which have soared in recent years, create most of the growth of high-wage jobs in America, and American service exports yielded a $60 billion trade surplus in 1992. Why would anyone want to trade this kind of performance and a 6.8% unemployment rate in the U.S. for a 10.3% unemployment rate in Europe, expected to grow to 12% by the end of 1994?

Rather than imitating Europe, which is more reluctant to change, or Japan, which is a racially homogeneous society, the U.S. should continue to lead these countries vigorously toward further openness and freer trade, especially in relations with the new democracies in Europe and developing countries, such as Mexico. Of course, the U.S. has to bargain tough with its trading partners. The real issues are 1) whether the U.S. bargains with a sense of its continuing economic strength or acts as if it is a victim of foreign commercial superiority and conspiracy, and 2) whether the goal remains freer global markets under common rules or becomes regional pacts that substitute for globalism, and bilateral pacts that predetermine results and restrict freedom.

ANTI-DEMOCRATIC FORCES

Success in integrating the new democracies into the industrial world is necessary to underpin a final principle of post-Cold War U.S. foreign policy—the need to contain persisting anti-democratic forces in the Balkans, Middle East and East Asia. U.S. power in these regions remains indispensable to protect freedom, just as it was to contain communism in Europe.

Ethnic and religious wars in the Balkans and Middle East threaten budding democracies in Hungary, Russia and other former communist states. A corrupt and paranoid communist government in North Korea husbands a secret nuclear weapons program and threatens South Korea's safety as well as Japan's long-term ability to remain non-nuclear and avoid a major military build-up that will destabilize all of Asia.

None of the authoritarian systems in the Balkans, Mideast and East Asia pose the immediate military threat that prompted containment in central Europe in the late 1940s. But all are dangerous. Ethnic cleansing in Bosnia can only encourage separatism and lawlessness in other hot spots of the former communist world, some more crucial to the balance of power, such as the Crimea or Ukraine. Humiliation of the United Nations in Europe weakens collective peacekeeping elsewhere (in Cambodia or Somalia) and sets back crucial U.N. efforts to contain the spread of nuclear weapons (in Ukraine, Iraq and Korea).

THE REAL CHOICE

Against such threats, the U.S. must lead. It should try to do so through the U.N., much as it led in the Cold War through NATO. But, as it did in the Cold and Gulf wars, it will have to be ready from time to time to push NATO and the U.N. to act more decisively, applying proportionate force along the lines recommended in the containment doctrine. The choice is not between the use of force and no force but between acting now or having to use more force later. If the U.S. fails to draw the line in Sarajevo today, can it hold the line in Macedonia tomorrow?

Successful foreign policy grows out of a sense of moral self-worth and corresponding leadership and strength in world affairs. America's self-worth requires steady progress toward a tolerant, multiethnic society at home, and its leadership abroad is both the surest guarantee against corrosive cynicism at home and the best defense of new democracies against old despots wherever the latter still threaten the worth and dignity of free individuals.

10 DEMOCRACY AND HUMAN RIGHTS

MESSIAH COMPLEX
CAN LEAD TO WAR

Vincent Kavaloski

Vincent Kavaloski is the Co-editor of Metanoia. *Metanoia, a newsletter of the Ecumenical Partnership for Peace and Justice of the Wisconsin Conference of Churches, seeks both to proclaim the prophetic vision of peace for our times and also to provide a creative forum for exploring pathways toward that vision.*

Points to Consider

1. Virtually every nation is sustained by a founding myth. How can the myth of nationalism, by combining a sense of superiority, together with a claim of divine destiny, justify war?

2. List and explain the three Biblical themes that create a potent but dangerous self-identity in the American psyche.

3. Explain from a religious point of view how the American myth of nationalism is blasphemous.

4. According to the author, how is the "myth of a nation-state" a lie?

Vincent Kavaloski, "How the Myth of Nationalism Leads to War," **Metanoia**, Winter 1990. Reprinted with permission.

Yea THOUGH I WaLK THrOUGH THe SHaDOW OF THe VaLLeY OF DeaTH, I SHaLL Fear no eviL, FOr I am crazY.

BOSNIA

CIVIL WAR

Cartoon by Richard Wright.

The myth of nationalism, by combining a sense of superiority, together with a claim to divine destiny, can and does justify war. It can even lead to genocide.

Virtually every nation is sustained by a founding myth, a shared story which explains why this particular people is special. Homer's *Iliad*, the great saga of the Trojan War, gave the ancient Greeks their sense of vast and heroic origins. Virgil's *Aenead*, inspired the Romans with a vision of empire: "to bear dominion over other nations, and to impose the law of peace." The British empire was sustained by the myth of the "white man's burden."

DIVINE DESTINY

Such foundation myths create a powerful and religious national identity, a mystical sense of "we-ness": "We have all come from one divine and heroic source, and we share one glorious destiny." But this very "we-ness" necessarily creates a "them." Those outside the group are viewed as not-special, or less than human, or as obstacles to the national destiny. Thus the myth of nationalism, by combining a sense of superiority, together with a claim to divine destiny, can and does justify war. It can even lead to genocide against the "other," just as Hitler's "myth of the master race" led to the ovens of Auschwitz. Indeed, most national myths cele-

EL MOZOTE MASSACRE

Chepe was 7 at the time, one of a group of children taken by the soldiers to a playing field near the school. He told Danner: "I didn't really understand what was happening until I saw a soldier take a kid he had been carrying—maybe 3 years old—throw him in the air and stab him with a bayonet. They slit some of the kids' throats, and many they hanged from the tree...The soldiers kept telling us, 'You are guerrillas and this is justice. This is justice.'"

The killers were from the U.S.-trained Atlacatl battalion. Their commanders, making a drive through territory where rebel forces had been, decided to kill everyone on the theory that the local population had nurtured the rebels. In fact, El Mozote was a stronghold of evangelical Christians, who were fiercely anti-Communist.

Anthony Lewis, **New York Times**, December 8, 1993.

brate military conquest as an essential part of their story.

The earliest American founding myth is strikingly different—on the face of it. It is a story of freedom-loving people fleeing the oppression and corruption of the "Old World" in order to found a "New World" built upon liberty and equality. We see here a creative combination of two Biblical themes: America as an innocent Eden; and the Exodus journey out of slavery.

But the American founding story also includes a third Biblical theme, America as Messiah. The "founding fathers" saw the new nation as "the depository of the sacred flame of liberty" (Jefferson) and hence it would lead the world toward freedom. The U.S. would be a "redeemer nation" for all humanity, the bearer of "manifest destiny."

DANGEROUS IDENTITY

The synthesis of these three Biblical themes created a potent but dangerous self-identity in the American psyche. On the one hand, we viewed ourselves as peaceful and innocent (Eden) as well as freedom-seeking (Exodus); on the other hand, we believed that we had the right—even duty—to "save the world" (Messiah

THE REAGAN ADMINISTRATION

The Reagan administration knew more than it publicly disclosed about some of the worst human rights abuses in El Salvador's civil war and withheld the information from Congress, declassified cables and interviews with former government officials indicate.

"Reagan Administration Knew of El Salvadorian Atrocities," **Star Tribune**, March 21, 1993.

theme) through our military and economic might. Thus Jefferson, who had written so movingly of American freedom, peace and democracy, went on as President to speak of the U.S. right to conquer Spanish-held lands "piece by piece."

The American historian, Ronald Wells, concludes that "the spiritual pride of the United States consisted in acting innocently upon the pretense of its special calling, despite the fact that it was almost constantly at war, either with the Indians at home, or with other nations..." After the War of Independence (1775-83) came the 1812-15 War with Britain, the 1846-48 War with Mexico, the 1861-65 Civil War, the 1898 War with Spain, World War I (1917-18), World War II (1941-45), Korea (1950-53) and Vietnam (1964-74). Add to these the wars of extermination against American Indians, the enslavement of millions of Black Africans, the almost one hundred military interventions in Latin America, countless CIA "covert actions" abroad, and military support for numerous repressive regimes around the world.

MYTH OVER REASON

Despite this historical record, most Americans continue to believe in the innocence and special destiny of the U.S. At one level, this demonstrates the power of myth over reason. An objective study of U.S. history would show that the government has acted much like other powerful nations in enforcing its will on its neighbors. Furthermore, the myth is logically self-contradictory: the innocence (Eden) and freedom-loving spirit (Exodus) which supposedly justify our "manifest destiny" abroad (Messiah complex) is actually contradicted by the military and economic coercion used to carry out that very destiny. The attempt to "impose" peace and freedom on other people by force is self-contradictory.

68

This is illustrated by President Cleveland's justification for the U.S. invasion of Cuba in 1898: "The U.S.," he wrote, (two years before the invasion) "is compelled to protect its own interests and those of its citizens, which are coincident with those of humanity generally, by resorting to such measures as will promptly restore to the Island the blessing of peace."

ABOVE THE LAW

From a theological point of view, the U.S. myth, like most myths of nationalism, is blasphemous. It portrays one nation as more "godly" than others, and hence above the moral law. It leads to what Senator Fulbright called the "arrogance of power"— an idolatrous worship of state power in the pursuit of "vital national interests" (the new name for "manifest destiny").

In this situation, the duty of people of faith is to call their country to repent of its pretensions. No nation is above the moral law, and no nation is exempt from judgment. In the final analysis, the myth of the nation-state is a lie because it denies the fundamental truth of the oneness of humanity: that we share not only a common human nature and a common creation, but also a common propensity toward sin, pride and error.

WHAT IS RELIGIOUS BIAS?

This activity may be used as an individualized study guide for students in libraries and resource centers or as a discussion catalyst in small group and classroom discussions.

Many readers are unaware that written material usually expresses an opinion or bias. The skill to read with insight and understanding requires the ability to detect different kinds of bias. **Political bias, race bias, sex bias, ethnocentric bias** and **religious bias** are five basic kinds of opinions expressed in editorials and literature that attempt to persuade. This activity will focus on **religious bias** defined in the glossary below.

FIVE KINDS OF EDITORIAL BIAS

sex bias – *the expression of dislike for and/or feeling of superiority over a person because of gender or sexual preference*

race bias – *the expression of dislike for and/or feeling of superiority over a racial group*

ethnocentric bias – *the expression of a belief that one's own group, race, religion, culture or nation is superior. Ethnocentric persons judge others by their own standards and values.*

political bias – *the expression of opinions and attitudes about government related issues on the local, state or international level*

religious bias – *the expression of a religious belief or attiitude*

70

Guidelines

Read through the following statements and decide which ones represent religious opinion or bias. Evaluate each statement by using the method indicated.

• **Place the letter *(R)* in front of any sentence that reflects *religious opinion or bias.***

• **Place the letter *(N)* in front of any sentence that does not reflect *religious opinion* or *bias*.**

• **Place the letter *(S)* in front of any sentence that you are not sure about.**

_____ 1. Religious leaders should oppose military intervention in all civil wars.

_____ 2. Corporations should be regulated by government agencies.

_____ 3. Religious traditions have left societies unprepared to deal wiith global militarism and war.

_____ 4. Religious leaders should not interfere wiith their political leaders' decisions about war and peace.

_____ 5. It is the responsibility of the churches to oppose other governments when they engage in violence and oppression.

_____ 6. The most serious problems in the world have a spiritual cause.

_____ 7. World hunger is a problem of technology and food shortages. It is not a spiritual question.

_____ 8. School prayer is a violation of the U.S. Constitution's provision for a separation between church and state.

_____ 9. Religion and politics should always be separate.

_____ 10. Religious people and leaders have a duty to organize resistance to political leaders who engage in war and violence.

CHAPTER 3

INTERVENTION AND GLOBAL SECURITY

11 INTERVENTION AND GLOBAL SECURITY

PREVENTING GLOBAL GENOCIDE

Jeane J. Kirkpatrick

Jeane J. Kirkpatrick is a Senior Fellow at the American Enterprise Institute in Washington, D.C.

Points to Consider:

1. Explain how the Vance/Owen plan divides Bosnia into ten ethnically distinct, autonomous provinces.

2. Discuss what effect the "peace plan" has on the people living in the Balkans.

3. How does the Clinton plan differ from the Vance/Owen plan?

4. Explain the role the United States should play in the Balkans.

Excerpted from congressional testimony by Jeane J. Kirkpatrick before the Senate Committee on Foreign Relations, February 18, 1993.

The plan is drawn on the principle that might makes right. Serbs are awarded most of the areas from which Muslims have been driven.

Even before he met with new U.S. Secretary of State Warren Christopher earlier this week, Lord David Owen, European Community negotiator for the Balkans, had charged that it was probably the fault of the United States that war still rages in Bosnia. The Clinton administration, he said, was giving hope to beleaguered Bosnian Muslims. That hope encouraged them to resist the "peace plan" developed by Owen and his co-chair Cyrus Vance, who serves as the U.N. Secretary General's special representative in the matter of the Balkans.

THE PEACE PLAN

It is easy to see why Bosnia's Muslims would resist. The Vance/Owen plan divides Bosnia into 10 ethnically distinct, autonomous provinces: three would be dominated by Croats (who make up 17 percent of the population), three by Muslims (who constituted 43 percent of the population before Serbian "ethnic cleansing" drove them from their homes), three by Serbians, and Sarajevo, the capital, would be jointly administered. The elected government of Bosnia (now headed by President Alija Izetbegovic) would be replaced on the signing of a cease-fire by a nine-person interim commission whose members would be equally drawn from each of the ethnic groups.

Only the Croats accepted the plan. Bosnian Serbs have been on again, off again about the plan since it was first presented. They want a corridor connecting Serbian enclaves to Serbia. Obviously Bosnian Muslims, who are the principal victims of Serbia's war, are also the big losers in this proposed peace settlement—in spite of Owen's declaration to the *London Financial Times* that "what has happened in the former Yugoslavia must be reversed...we are not going to have the Muslims treated like the Jews once were in Europe."

The Vance/Owen plan rewards "ethnic cleansing" by legitimizing Serb control of land from which Muslims have been driven. It also rewards Croats who are just now moving militarily to consolidate control over lands assigned to them under the Vance/Owen plan—on grounds that Muslim extremists and fundamentalists threaten the national identity of the Croatian community in

Cartoon by Richard Wright.

Bosnia. At the same time Croats are seeking to reclaim by force Serbian enclaves in Croatia set up in the cease-fire negotiated under U.N. auspices. "We will liberate the last inch of Croatia from Serbian Chetnike occupation," said Croatian President, Franjo Tudjman.

Events in Croatia have not caused Vance and Owen to doubt that their peace plan for Bosnia can end the fighting—if it is imposed by the U.N. Security Council. President Clinton, said Owen "should stop all of this loose talk about using force, make it clear to Izetbegovic that he's got no real alternative to these negotiations...then provide American troops as part of a NATO force."

"Please don't do it," pleads Bosnia's president.

The plan is drawn on the principle that might makes right. Serbs are awarded most of the areas from which Muslims have been driven. Serbs are given political representation far beyond their numbers. The legitimate Bosnian government is dismantled. The democratically adopted constitution is scrapped. Haris Silajdzic, Bosnia's foreign minister, did not exaggerate in saying, "We, as a member of the United Nations, will never accept the abolition of our constitution, our legality, which is based on free and democratic elections."

75

EMPOWER AMERICA

How does President Clinton decide which campaign promises to keep? Candidate Clinton called for determined American action—if necessary—to end Serbian violence and ethnic cleansing. But President Clinton has announced his support for the deeply flawed Vance/Owen peace process.

Candidate Clinton demanded that Serbia's heavy weapons be put under U.N. supervision, and that Bosnian refugees be permitted to return to their homes. But President Clinton has concluded that ethnic cleansing cannot be reversed, and has embraced a plan that permits Serbs to keep conquered Bosnian territories.

Candidate Clinton promised that continued Serbian interference with relief convoys would be met with U.S. air strikes. But President Clinton merely "urges" that aid be permitted to flow to those in desperate need. Candidate Clinton, "outraged" by the revelations of concentration camps in Bosnia, called for "collective action, including the use of force, if necessary," to stop the killing in these camps. But President Clinton does not mention the 70,000 to 100,000 prisoners in Serbian concentration camps.

As if that weren't bad enough, President Clinton seems to have promised American ground troops to help enforce the gains of ethnic cleansing. Introducing thousands of peacekeepers where there is no peace will prove an expensive, ineffective, possibly dangerous substitute for effective action.

The Clinton plan is not as bad as the Vance/Owen plan. It distinguishes between the aggressor and the victim and it names the aggressor. That's progress. It proposes to enforce the no-fly zone, by force if necessary. It rejects the suggestion that the Vance/Owen plan be imposed on the parties by force, if necessary. It promises to tighten the notoriously ineffective embargo on Serbia.

Like Candidate Clinton, President Clinton recognizes that vitally important issues of conscience, of strategic interests, and of international law are at stake in Bosnia. The solution proposed by the Clinton administration is no solution. It does not create an international standard for the fair treatment of minorities. It does not strengthen institutions of collective security. It does not raise the price for aggression. It should be rethought.

Unfortunately in this first important action in foreign policy,

President Clinton sacrifices the principles invoked by Candidate Clinton to a policy of appeasement which will prove no more successful than previous efforts to appease aggressors.

CONCLUSION

The European Community and the United Nations have demanded an end to ethnic cleansing, and an end to attacks on civilians. They have demanded cooperation of all parties to permit the delivery of humanitarian assistance to Sarajevo and other parts of Bosnia-Herzegovina. They have called for a no-fly zone. But ethnic cleansing has continued and the no-fly zone has not been enforced. Humanitarian assistance for Bosnian towns has not been permitted to reach starving Bosnians.

And, proving that Milosevic's Greater Serbia is as large as his ambition, Serbian repression of the population of Kosovo is underway and over two hundred thousand have already fled from this land Milosevic claims for Serbia. Such men do not negotiate "political" solutions. They just go on expanding their power until they encounter an overwhelming counter force.

That being the case, what should the United States do?

First, deliver humanitarian assistance, by force if necessary.

Second, enforce the no-fly ban over Bosnia.

Third, secure the immediate release of Bosnians and Croatians held in concentration camps.

Fourth, demand the right of refugees to return to their homes. Restore to former owners property seized by force during "ethnic cleansing."

If it seems desirable and feasible, a new resolution specifically authorizing the use of all necessary means could be passed by the U.N. Security Council. If not, help could be offered under Article 51 as self-defense and collective self-defense. Then and only then might it make sense to introduce U.N. peacekeepers into the region. Until then sharply focused airpower should prove more useful.

What I advocate for Bosnia is what President Bill Clinton advocated when he was a candidate. Clinton should reread his old speeches. They recognized that like Saddam Hussein, Milosevic and his friends are very dangerous but not legally insane. If the price of aggression is high enough, they will cease aggression.

12 INTERVENTION AND GLOBAL SECURITY

SAY "NO" TO BOSNIAN INTERVENTION

Harvey F. Egan

Harvey F. Egan is pastor emeritus of St. Joan of Arc Catholic Church in Minneapolis, Minnesota.

Points to Consider:

1. How does the author describe war?

2. Do citizens have a right to say "no" when the United States says "kill?"

3. What might happen in America if we go to war in Bosnia?

Harvey F. Egan, "Before We Plunge Again Into War," **Star Tribune**, 1994. Reprinted with permission from **Star Tribune**, Minneapolis.

Does a citizen have a right to say "No!" when the government says "Kill!"?

War is violence run amok, murder on a massive scale—immoral, insane, ungodly, inhuman, expensive, futile, inconclusive. Normal persons believe the killing of a person is evil, sinful, brutal, tragic. Thus says God, her prophets, every book of ethics, every sensitive human heart and all mainline religions.

We are currently being softened up for entrance into another war. Pentagon officials and the makers of weapons, needing a war every decade, are cunningly working to push us into a maelstrom in the Balkans, "a Bosch-like tapestry of interlocking ethnic rivalries."

Soon the United States military brass will beckon young men and women and tell them they must go to Bosnia and fight for humanity or decency or moral integrity or whatever the word will be this time. Soon conformity to the military machine will be compulsory, a salute will become sacramental, a conscientious objector will be considered a traitor. Thus patriotism doth make puppets of us all, a nation of poorer, weaker, sadder citizens. Flag-waving will be followed by carnage beyond control, wounds that will not heal, corpses beyond counting, terrorism as rampant as racism.

Some doubts have recently surfaced, some questions should now be asked.

What happened to those noble plans for a new world order?

Do we remember the lies that seduced us into past wars?

Why do we protest distant violence and tolerate nearby injustice?

Does anyone know how to change a volcanic jungle into a peaceful garden?

Are we pledged to prevent all ethnic cleansing and correct morally corrupt and incompetent governments?

Since every war is eventually terminated by negotiations, why not initiate negotiations before the killings?

Are we stubborn in diplomatic procedures?

Can weapons inspire persons to cultivate higher values?

Cartoon by Mike Ramirez. Reprinted with permission of **Copley News Service.**

Who has designated us to be a policeman for the world, a killer of foreign culprits?

Can anyone clearly, wisely and convincingly tell us what American interests are at stake in the Bosnian debacle?

What will be the specific terms, short-range and long-range, of a possible military intervention in Bosnia?

Should not the hesitancy of European nations "to take measures quickly and decisively" against Bosnia's Serbs give us more pause than belligerence?

Will most European nations reluctantly endure a takeover by the Serbs rather than engage in military intervention?

Can we obtain an international coalition to help solve "a problem from hell?"

Will our allies again hold our coats as American troops do the fighting?

Why should the United States be the leader of a march toward a possible Armageddon?

If we are inclined to take military action, will we obtain the necessary resolutions of approval from the United Nations and the U.S. Congress?

Would an American unilateral decision to plunge into military intervention alone have any chance of solving the problems?

Is blind support of a president perfect or perverse democracy?

For wisdom in making a war-involving decision, will Congress consult the full rank and file of American citizens?

In a threat of war, will American citizens consult the law of God and the conscience of the human family?

Will air strikes be a prologue to a dispatch of ground troops?

Will the conflict spill beyond Bosnia's borders to trigger an irreversible escalation of violence leading to World War III?

Does anyone believe surgical air strikes are precise?

Will we bomb villages and hospitals again?

What assurances can we give that children, women, the ailing and elderly will not be killed?

As aggression increases, will peacekeepers become targets?

In lands where hatreds prevail with primitive ferocity, are there any secure places?

In making a military onslaught against a population of several ethnic groups, can friends be distinguished from foes?

Will the struggle end only when one ethnic group is exterminated?

Who can design and build a proper and workable political structure for nations after the annihilation of their society?

What groups are pushing a president, a reluctant warrior, to initiate military action?

If we go to war, will the critical needs of our nation—health care, environmental protection, deficit reduction, school improvements, urban rebuilding—be indefinitely postponed?

Will we recognize the continuing causes of war in our midst—greed, competitiveness, racism, poverty, hedonism, addictions, etc.—and work energetically to cure these ailments?

Has our indulgence in excessive luxuries turned our nation to excessive violence?

FOREIGN INTERVENTION

The president, James Polk, had, in Grant's judgment, the ulterior motive of annexing Texas, already separated from Mexico. "I was bitterly opposed to the measure," Grant wrote, "and to this day regard the war which resulted as one of the most unjust ever waged by a stronger against a weaker nation."

William S. McFeely, "A Lesson in Intervention from Ulysses S. Grant," **Star Tribune**, December 19, 1984, p. 25A.

Is not every expression of racism and sexism an act of war?

Is not every handgun at home an invitation to wage war?

Will a fireside chat convince many Americans to go to war?

Does a citizen have a right to say "No!" when the government says "Kill!"?

Are people aware that the "just war" theology has been repudiated?

Will millions of enlightened, conscientious Americans resist the propulsion toward madness and murder?

Will we come to realize that the life and integrity of every person in the world is infinitely precious?

When will we learn that the killing of persons makes us savages?

Will unanswered questions provoke a massive resistance and lead us to rationality, restraint and peace?

13 INTERVENTION AND GLOBAL SECURITY

INTERVENTION MUST COME EARLY

Carol Birkland

Carol Birkland of the Lutheran World Federation staff in Geneva offers this reflection on the current chaos and suffering in Somalia and the former Yugoslavia, and what might be considered to prevent such situations.

Points to Consider:

1. What problem do many aid agencies find themselves caught between when trying to intervene?

2. Why has helping people in need become such a "risky business?"

3. What does Erskine Childers feel is necessary for successful intervention?

4. What are the two alternatives once shooting starts, and the situation disintegrates into irrationality?

Carol Birkland, "Preventative Diplomacy and the New World Order," **Sequoia**, January/February 1993.

To what extent can the world community stand by and watch governments torture, intentionally starve, or forcibly relocate citizens under the protective umbrella of their appeal to state sovereignty?

Helping those in need in today's world has become an increasingly risky business. More and more it seems that trying to aid victims caught in the cross fire of civil conflicts means that those attempting to deliver the aid are themselves caught in the cross fire.

An Italian plane, carrying aid to the besieged city of Sarajevo in Bosnia-Herzegovina, was shot down; the United Nations recalled its aid workers from southern Sudan after three were killed; and one can only marvel that there has not been more death and injury to those delivering aid into the chaos of Somalia.

INTERVENTION

Aid agencies—both governmental and [CARE, Red Cross, etc.]—find themselves caught between their commitment to provide aid and their desire to safeguard their mostly-defenseless employees and volunteer workers. They are also beginning to ask questions about whether or not they have the right to intervene (by force of arms, if necessary) in situations of extreme human need; whether or not existing international humanitarian law gives civilian victims "the human right" to receive aid; and finally, in situations where a government refuses to allow access to victims, do aid agencies have the right to violate that state's sovereignty in order to deliver aid?

According to Larry Minear, co-director of the Humanitarianism and War project at Brown University [and son of Paul Minear, New Testament professor emeritus of Yale Divinity School—editor's note], the right to receive humanitarian assistance does exist and is found in various U.N. covenants and in the Geneva Conventions and Protocols. International humanitarian law provides that aid, which is impartial in character and conducted without any adverse distinction, should not be seen by any government as an unfriendly act or interference.

However, according to Additional Protocol I of 1977, Article 70, relief actions are "subject to the agreement of the Parties concerned." One wonders how such an agreement could be

reached, for example, between the seven factions/clans fighting for ultimate control in Somalia.

In fact, it is in situations like Somalia where questions concerning violations of state sovereignty seem almost extraneous. Certainly issues related to state sovereignty must continue to inform international relations, but to what extent can the world community stand by and watch governments torture, intentionally starve, or forcibly relocate citizens under the protective umbrella of their appeal to state sovereignty? This is especially the case when a particular government's grip on the reins of sovereignty is, at best, a slippery one.

PREVENTION

The discussions concerning "humanitarian intervention" are more and more moving toward talk of "prevention." Unlike the situation where aid and protection was provided to the Kurds against the wishes of Iraq, the lessons of Somalia and Yugoslavia are that unarmed relief workers are no match for heavily armed forces intent on "fighting it out to the bitter end."

Upon the invitation of the U.N. Security Council, Secretary-General Boutros Boutros-Ghali recently prepared a report entitled, "An Agenda for Peace: Preventive Diplomacy, Peacemaking and Peace-keeping." In the third chapter of that report the Secretary-

STRATEGIC INDEPENDENCE

A policy of strategic independence is based on a more modest and sustainable security role for the United States and on a realistic assessment of the post-Cold War international system.

The new strategy would make it possible to defend America's security interests with a military force of approximately 900,000 active duty personnel—compared with the current force of some 2 million and the force of 1.6 million contemplated by the Pentagon for the mid-1990s. A policy of strategic independence would enable the United States to reduce its military budget from the current $291 billion a year to approximately $125 billion a year (measured in 1991 dollars) over a five-year period. The beneficial economic impact of a "peace dividend" of that magnitude, if returned to the American people in the form of tax reductions, would be enormous.

After those reductions, the United States would still be spending three times as much on the military as any other G-7 member. The reductions seem radical only in the context of the bloated Cold War era military budgets that have come to be considered "normal."

Excerpted from Ted Galen Carpenter, "The Case for United States Strategic Independence," a Foreign Policy Briefing paper from the CATO Institute, January 16, 1992.

General states that, "the most desirable and efficient employment of diplomacy is to ease tensions before they result in conflict—or, if conflict breaks out, to act swiftly to contain it and resolve its underlying causes."

One wonders what might have happened, for example, if in Somalia such preventive diplomacy mechanisms had both been in place and applied. What would have happened if preventive action had been taken before heavily armed clans were able to fill the power vacuum created when the dictator Barre fled?

Could the clans have been disarmed as a prelude to devising some kind of peaceful power-sharing arrangement? Or, even once the shooting started—but before the rivals were able to solidify their organizations—could an armed U.N. force have

87

been "preventively deployed" in the hope of forcing stabilization?

Obviously there are no answers to these questions. However, the chaos and tragedy now being played out in both Somalia and the former Yugoslavia should underscore the critical importance of the questions. Erskine Childers, a retired U.N. official now working on a Dag Hammarskjold and Ford Foundation research project aimed at reorganizing the U.N., has said that "the size of each crisis is directly increased by the lack of early action." Childers stresses the need for fact-finding, mediation, and only if absolutely necessary, intervention.

The kind of preventive diplomacy that both Childers and Boutros-Ghali advocate will require a high degree of international cooperation and can only be achieved if the world, as a whole, has the collective will to attempt to solve conflict in a new way.

ALTERNATIVES

If there is one thing that the tragedies of Yugoslavia and Somalia should have taught, it is that after the shooting starts and the situation disintegrates into irrationality, there is less and less that humanitarian agencies can do to alleviate suffering—especially if the combatants have no hesitation to shoot at and kill aid workers.

At that point there are two alternatives: STAY, which increasingly means dodging bullets to guard the relief aid; or LEAVE— which unfortunately more and more agencies may be forced to do. There has to be a THIRD alternative.

14 INTERVENTION AND GLOBAL SECURITY

PAX AMERICANA — CAN PEACE BE IMPOSED?

Russel Kirk

Russel Kirk, president of two educational foundations, is the author of thirty books and the editor of Conservative Thought *(Transaction Publishers).*

Points to Consider:

1. Discuss whether or not military domination is the only means for building an American empire.

2. Upon what assumption is "swift and beneficent establishment of American democratic capitalism" founded?

3. Why are the "blessings of America" difficult to export?

4. How does the author define the *Pax Americana?*

Russel Kirk, "Pax Americana — Can America Impose Peace?" **Special Report** Number 62 of Public Policy Education Fund, Inc., 161 E. Pine St., Grove City, PA 16127, September 1991. Reprinted with permission.

"The American Constitution is not for export." Our American advantages are the product of peculiar historical circumstances.

More than seven decades ago, President Woodrow Wilson busied himself in rearranging the map of Europe and planning for perpetual peace, worldwide. Presidents Woodrow Wilson, Franklin Roosevelt, and Lyndon Johnson strove for American domination of the world. President George Bush emulated those eminent Democrats. Out of mixed motives, he embarked upon a course of massive and forceful intervention in the region of the Persian Gulf. His decision to strike Iraq with overwhelming power may lead to other high deeds abroad—resulting, just possibly, in a Pax Americana comparable to the old Pax Romana; but resulting more probably in an American hegemony over every continent—a domination costly and difficult to maintain...

I. ONE VIEW OF PAX AMERICANA

It seems to be the intention of some American strategists to develop an American empire made up of client states, after the Roman fashion—client states based upon the existing models of Israel, El Salvador, Grenada, Kuwait, the Philippines and (formerly) Lebanon. Militarily, Japan is a client state. Fiscally, several other countries already are client states—among them Zaire, ruled by the ghastly tyrant Mobutu, despite State Department professions of a kind of religion of democracy. Is a time at hand when the sun will never set on the Stars and Stripes, flown from the flagposts of American military and naval bases?...

A New World Order, an artificial universal democracy, with no better footing than American military might, would dissolve swiftly as did American power in Vietnam...

Military domination is not the only means for building an American empire...This whole concept of swift establishment of American "democratic capitalism" universally is founded upon the assumption that all peoples will readily and rapidly embrace American political and social forms—quite as the Russian Communists, for seven decades, assumed that all the world would come to accept happily Marxist political and social forms. This confusion has been made worse by a loose employment of such terms as "freedom" and "democracy." The truth is that "liberal democracy" is a body of institutions of nineteenth century origins,

It is our nation's duty to protect the whole world.

Cartoon by Darren Brettingen.

almost peculiar to western Europe and the English-speaking nations. Liberal democracy remains largely incomprehensible and unattainable, in the short run, in most of the "Third World" states.

II. EXPORTING U.S. BLESSINGS?

The Difficulties—The United States of America has enjoyed blessings, but those blessings are of a nature difficult to export...As Dr. Daniel Boorstin, one of our wiser living historians, puts the matter, "The American Constitution is not for export." Our American advantages are the product of peculiar historical circumstances in large part...

The intended translation of American institutions to Africa has been a dismal failure: Africa has obdurately insisted upon remaining African. Not one liberal democracy exists in "emergent" Africa, nor is there any prospect of such development. *(Editor's Note: South Africa now has a democratic government.)* The one country that was founded in emulation of American ways, Liberia, has collapsed into a ghastly anarchy. The United States is denounced in many African countries as the menacing new imperialist power. No large-scale industrialization has come to pass in "emergent" Africa; on the contrary, in most of that continent agriculture and mining have sadly declined since independence. Constitutionalism is a sham in nearly all African states; squalid new oligarchs supplant tribal chiefs; the military junta and the monolithic repressive party stand triumphant...

I venture to suggest that it would be highly imprudent for the government of the United States, in the name of some New World Order or Democratic Capitalism, to set about undermining regimes that do not seem perfectly democratic to the editors of the *New York Times*, say—whether that undermining be worked through the suasion and the money of the Endowment for Democracy, or through the CIA and military operations.

"Four legs good, two legs bad"—such is the ideology of the pigs in *Animal Farm*. "Democracy good, all else bad"—such is the democratist ideology. A politicized American army operating abroad would be no more popular than the Red Army has been. An imposed abstract "democracy" thrust upon peoples unprepared for it would produce at first anarchy, then rule by force and a master. The differing nations of our time must find their own several ways to order and justice and freedom. The Americans have not been appointed their keepers. It is not the American government that could bring into being a Pax Americana: only the American people, who, working in ways nonpolitical, might persuade other peoples to benefit from our example.

PACIFIC ISLANDERS

This 20th-century colonialism is manifest in the story of Palau. Under its U.N. mandate, the United States was to foster economic and political development in the islands, the end being self-sufficiency and self-government. But 43 years and millions of dollars later, Palau is an economic dependency, rich in resources but without developed agricultural or fishing enterprises, without a small productive sector, heavily indebted and reliant on the U.S. government for about 90 percent of its annual budget.

JoAnn Wypijewski, "Islanders Challenge U.S. Cold War Goals," **Star Tribune**, March 5, 1990.

The Costliness of Empire—By meddling, with good intentions, in the affairs of distant lands, empires have been created in a fit of absence of mind. So it was that the Roman Republic became the Roman Empire. Roman peace-keeping garrisons were stationed in remote regions; the cultures of those remote regions decayed sadly, under Roman dominion. Increasingly the resources of the Empire were dissipated by the enormous expense of policing the known civilized world; and the economy virtually collapsed under the burden of taxation.

That ruinous process seems to have begun for America already. American troops remain in the region of the Persian Gulf months after American victory there, and American officials negotiate for permanent bases. "Desert Shield" and "Desert Storm" cost the federal treasury a billion dollars per day, at the lowest estimate: that is, for the two months of Shield and Storm, a total of at least sixty billion dollars ($60,000,000,000). In empires, over-expansion of military commitments and political administration soon becomes a running sore: the homelands may be drained dry by taxation. So it was with the Pax Romana...

III. AMERICA AS AN EXAMPLE — BEGINNING AT HOME

No, a Pax Americana is conceivable only so far as the United States, without aspiring to dominate the world, instead offers the

93

world an example, a model of ordered freedom — for possible emulation. Setting an example is very different from bullying one's neighbors or from bribing them. In an age of ferocious ideologies and fantastic political schemes, the United States may offer a model of the just society, reconciling the claims of order and the claims of freedom and settling for politics as the art of the possible.

15 INTERVENTION AND GLOBAL SECURITY

WHEN MILITARY INTERVENTION IS NECESSARY

Lynne Jones

Dr. Lynne Jones is a psychiatrist and writer who has lived and traveled extensively in Eastern Europe and the former Yugoslavia in the last ten years. She is former chairperson of British European Nuclear Disarmament (END) and is currently working with Bosnian refugees in Slovenia.

Points to Consider:

1. What crimes are being committed in Bosnia?

2. Under what circumstances should a nation undertake military intervention?

3. Explain the peace movement's attitude toward military intervention.

4. How does the author explain the new model for military intervention?

Lynne Jones, "The Peace Movement's Moral Failure in Bosnia," **Peace and Democracy News**, Summer 1993.

It is quite clear that a terrible crime is being committed under our noses.

What to do about Bosnia? For the first time in my life I am faced with a horrifying war that is neither historically nor geographically distant and for which there appears to be no clear or obvious solution. In 1982 I helped to organize a demonstration of 30,000 women outside Greenham Common Airbase. And like many of the others in that circle of hope and empowerment, I became quite skilled at explaining the miseries of a post-nuclear world: the breakdown of law and order, unchecked epidemics, no water, no electricity, operations without anaesthetic, starvation, and freezing cold. I argued in court that such weapons were genocidal and their use would be a war crime.

Yet ten years later the image of encirclement is no longer associated in my mind with that joyous and life-affirming group of women but with heavy artillery that mercilessly bombards a civilian population to death, and I have to recognize that as a peace movement we failed. Not just because nuclear weapons continue to exist, proliferate, and endanger us all, but because in anticipating and working to prevent the imagined holocaust of the third world war, we did nothing to prevent a more limited holocaust on our doorstep...

If we argue, at this juncture, against military intervention or against lifting the arms embargo imposed on the Bosnian government and its supporters, we have a moral responsibility to come up with alternatives to stop the torture, killings, mass rape, and bombardment. I long to hear what these are, for I can think of none myself, and what I have read so far offers little comfort.

First, there are friends who, in what must be quite unique concordance with the British government, view this as a "civil war," based on long-standing ethnic animosities, in which all parties are equally guilty and about which nothing can be done, except to offer hot tea, bandages, and "talks." There is no doubt that all sides are committing atrocities. But there is also no doubt that the Serbs, in their conflict with most other ethnic groups in the regions, are the main aggressor and responsible for the worst crimes.

"A DIFFERENT LOGIC"

War Resisters International (WRI) and the International

Reprinted with permission from **Star Tribune**, Minneapolis.

Fellowship of Reconciliation (IFOR) argued, in a June 1992 statement, against military intervention in Bosnia, that "any use of military force introduces a different logic" with the subsequent risk of escalation and creates a dangerous precedent for the solution of conflict in the New World Order. Yet surely a military logic of a very vicious kind has already been introduced, it is already escalating, and the precedent set by allowing the violence to continue and profit unchecked is equally dangerous. They recommended nonviolent social defense, modestly refraining from specifying what such tactics should be. Yet even prominent theoreticians in the field acknowledge the paucity of nonviolent tactics in the face of genocide and mass deportations. The normal "weapons" of noncooperation have no meaning in dealing with a group that has no interest in your cooperation but is bent upon your destruction. Escape is, of course, one possibility, but in the siege of Bosnian cities even that option is closed. Interestingly, when in the winter of 1993 the citizens of Sarajevo adopted the nonviolent tactic of an "aid boycott"—an imaginative adaptation of the hunger strike—in order to expose the hypocrisy of Western relief efforts and to push for effective humanitarian assistance to the besieged in Eastern Bosnia, they were roundly condemned.

WRI and IFOR then list a variety of nonviolent interventions to extend and develop the peace process that fail to address the substantial issue of how to protect a civilian population from slaughter while the "peace process" continues, or how to enforce its implementation once agreement is reached. My own view of the peace process in its current form is that the "ethnic" solution being imposed on Bosnia will be a source of endless war and has already provided the impetus and justification for another horrifying round of "ethnic cleansing," by both Serbs and Croats...

KNEE-JERK ANTI-INTERVENTIONISM

Some sections of the peace movement have a knee-jerk "anti-intervention" position that is based on a long experience of observing the continuing catastrophic consequences of superpower involvement in the Third World: we point to Vietnam, Central America, Afghanistan, the Middle East, and rightly reject the hypocrisy of wrapping strategic and economic interests in the shroud of a bogus concern for human rights. The paradox is that, preoccupied as we were by the stereotype of this kind of large-scale military intervention, we failed to challenge those political interventions that helped create this mess in the first place. These include: the West's unequivocal support for the maintenance of an integral Yugoslavia at any price and its failure to support the confederal solution suggested by Slovenia, Croatia, Bosnia-Herzegovina, and Macedonia; the West's refusal to push for democratization or human rights, thus allowing Milosevic to act with impunity against the Kosovars; the West's continued dealings with the "federal" government of Yugoslavia as if it represented the whole federation long after all federal institutions had collapsed, and it was clear that it only represented Belgrade...

PACIFISM

This brings me to the vexed question for pacifists: should military force be used? The fundamental principle at stake is that human lives are of equal value and that therefore one life cannot be taken to save another. This means one is pushed to develop nonviolent means to protect life and human dignity when they are threatened. However, so far, we have failed to come up with a nonviolent strategy to prevent the extermination of a whole people. To do nothing in this situation is to say that these lives are not worth being saved. That is to say that Muslim lives are not of equal value to those carrying out the killing from the hills. My

Doability, however is only the first requirement for intervention. Intervention must be not just doable but also worth doing. National interest is one justification for armed intervention. Is humanitarianism? At what point does a violation of humanitarian norms become so extraordinary as to justify, indeed morally compel, military intervention?

At the point of genocide. All such distinctions must be somewhat arbitrary, but since lines must be drawn, we might as well make them bright.

Charles Krauthammer, "When Should U.S. Intervene?" **The Washington Post,** December 1992.

point is not to argue that force must be used to stop this. I simply believe that while we cannot come up with alternatives, I have no right to argue against the use of force by others, whether this is in the form of different kinds of military intervention or through the provision of access to arms for self defense. And it is certainly completely immoral to deny both.

FUNDAMENTALISM

A fundamentalist attachment to principle is of no use to me if it gets in the way of the objects such a principle was meant to serve: namely, people's right to life. I am against war; that is why I wish to stop it. The fact is that even limited actions—such as effective sanctions, a genuine air exclusion zone, secure corridors for the delivery of humanitarian relief, or the arrest and trial of war criminals—are impossible without at least the threat of force. And to regard the force necessary to end an aggressive war as morally equivalent to that used to expel or exterminate another human group is a form of moral reductionism of the worst kind. The immediate consequence is that the war of aggression continues.

LIFTING THE ARMS EMBARGO IS NOT ENOUGH

Lifting the arms embargo is morally appealing not simply because we have no right to deprive people of the means to defend their lives but because of the moral distance it can create, thus providing comfort to those pacifists who hold the "I don't approve of their methods but it's not my place to dictate" position. I myself have taken a similar position in the past, but now I am no longer sure that it is not in fact another kind of moral cheating and, on its own, an irresponsible recommendation. This is because, first, it now seems clear that logistically it would be very difficult to get arms to the Bosnian government forces in the places required in the quantities needed for a definitive and speedy victory. Thus what we would actually be proposing is a long and bloody war of position in which thousands more lives would be lost and the country utterly devastated.

Thus my own choice would be to offer the Bosnian government military support under their control rather than to offer arms. This would avoid the danger of superpower "solutions" from outside, with all the attendant risks of creating a fourth side in the conflict and the danger of the intervening force staying longer than wanted. I would also suggest that the genuine threat of confronting a well-organized and clearly superior force might be sufficient to bring about a ceasefire immediately with no further loss of life. I do not know if this would happen, but is this more risky than going on as before?

A NEW MODEL FOR INTERVENTION

Such action could provide a new model for international intervention. Such a force should itself be truly international. The mandatory duties and limits of such action should be set in a clear legal framework. For example U.N. forces acting under Bosnian government control could not be ordered to commit acts of revenge or war crimes. This is not what happens at the moment, whatever the rhetoric, but the only way to move from imperialist interventions for strategic interest to just interventions on behalf of human rights is not to condemn intervention per se but to try to reform the structures we have available at the moment, most significantly the U.N. This is the beginning of a much longer discussion. My main point is that while we do not have the ideal institutions to act on Bosnia's behalf, we still have the responsibility, and pushing for a just and limited intervention under their own government's control might help in itself to create the framework and institutions we need.

Nor do I believe that saying force may be needed to stop extermination now precludes me from working at the same time for those measures that might prevent such horrors arising in the future: social justice, and regional and global demilitarization. To argue that it does is like saying that support for the right to abortion precludes a campaign for free, safe, effective contraception. There are situations where prevention has failed and the choice between evils is evil. Not choosing is our privilege. We do not have the right to choose for Bosnia.

MILITARY INTERVENTION: NOT FOR ME

Stephen R. Shalom

Stephen R. Shalom teaches political science at William Paterson College in New Jersey. He writes for Z Magazine and is a board member of the Campaign for Peace and Democracy.

Points to Consider:

1. Explain the author's basic case against foreign intervention.

2. Explain each of the four arguments the author makes in opposition to military intervention.

3. How is military intervention different from foreign trade and foreign aid in international relations?

4. According to the author, how important is intervention with a caring motivation when dealing with the Haitian people?

Stephen R. Shalom, "Military Intervention, Not for Me," **The Nonviolent Activist,** September/October, 1994. Reprinted with permission.

Those concerned about peace and justice should continue to oppose U.S. interventions in general.

Everyone on the Left agrees that we should oppose bad U.S. military intervention abroad. An increasing number of Left voices, however, are now urging that we should support "good" interventions.

I am going to argue that those concerned about peace and justice should continue to oppose U.S. interventions in general. I do not advance this as an absolute principle, but as an extremely strong presumption. My basic case against U.S. intervention has four components: (1) by making good interventions possible, we make bad interventions more likely (the precedent argument); (2) bad countries don't make good interventions; (3) outsiders are inherently incapable of bringing self-determination to others (as argued by John Stuart Mill); and (4) the pacifist argument that military force is counterproductive.

FOUR ARGUMENTS

The precedent argument holds that even if there were a good intervention, it would serve to weaken the taboo against intervention in general. Obviously, there have been many other violations of this taboo before, but there remains a reasonably widespread consensus against foreign intervention. For the Left to endorse the precedent of interventions, even for a good cause, may well help open the floodgates to many other bad interventions. Likewise, to develop or maintain the capabilities to undertake good interventions, one has to build up the same Pentagon budget, the same interventionary weapons systems, and the same foreign base structure that are used for and facilitate bad interventions.

My *second* argument against intervention is that bad countries are not likely to undertake good interventions. Even if the U.S. decides to intervene in some case where the Left agrees that evil is being done, the government will act so as to further its own interests, not those of the local victims.

A *third* argument against intervention is one that goes back to at least John Stuart Mill: members of a political community cannot be set free by an external force. It Is by the very process of strug gling to become free by their own efforts that people develop the qualities they need for maintaining freedom. Related to this argument is another liability that outsiders have in bringing freedom to

Cartoon by Kirk Anderson.

others: outsiders are often uninformed of local conditions and thus ill-suited to bring social benefit.

The *fourth* argument against intervention is the pacifist critique of military action. In many ways, military action undermines the values we hope to promote, and thus undermines democracy. The means one uses to attain certain ends invariably influences the ends that are actually achieved. Moreover, military action almost never deals with the root causes of problems and thus using it encourages quick fix solutions that ignore the underlying sources of conflict...

MILITARY INTERVENTION IS DIFFERENT

But from the fact that some sort of intervention in trade and aid policy is inevitable, it does not follow that military intervention is justified. Trade and aid are the normal, legal practices of international life. Every country has the right to decide who it wants to trade with or aid, and in deciding it is inevitably rewarding or penalizing other countries. But sending in the Marines is not the same thing. Countries do not normally have the right to invade other countries. Generally, it is not intervention to fail to dispatch troops. So there is nothing inconsistent with a position that says that U.S. trade and aid policy should favor human rights, democracy, and adherence to international law, while at the same time

> ## NO TO INTERVENTION
>
> I will argue that intervention as I define it is never good foreign policy, no matter how appealing the overall humanitarian case seems to be for changing political structure. Even if the intervening side has overwhelming military superiority, it rarely works, and its failure invariably leaves the target society worse off than if the internal play of forces had been allowed to run its course, however destructive and brutal.
>
> Richard Falk, "Hard Choices and Tragic Dilemmas," **The Nation**, December 20, 1993.

the U.S. should not engage in military intervention...

Those who favor U.S. intervention to prevent some evil in the world ought to ask themselves whether they would favor calling for Russian intervention in Haiti or Bosnia. If not, why not? It can't be because the Russians have been qualitatively more aggressive in their foreign policy than the U.S., nor that Russian foreign policy is significantly less under democratic control than that of the U.S. (whose invasions of Panama and Grenada, its mining of Nicaraguan harbors, etc. were wholly undemocratic)...

It seems clear that any U.S. or NATO intervention in Bosnia would be for the purpose of imposing a settlement that ratifies Serbian aggression and ethnic cleansing, for it is inconceivable that Washington, London, or Paris would intervene to achieve any purposes other than those they have been seeking by means short of military intervention. Their purposes are made clear by the Security Council-imposed arms embargo (which denies Bosnia the right to self-defense in behalf of its multi-ethnic democracy), and by all the partition plans. Countries that resist lifting the arms embargo are obviously not going to send in troops to push back the Serbs. Countries that endorse partition are not going to re-establish a multi-ethnic Bosnia by force of arms.

HAITI'S SAVIOUR?

In Haiti, the U.S. has supported the status quo for decades because it served U.S. interests to do so. When Aristide was elected, the U.S. did what it could to undermine him and to funnel support to the Haitian military which was Washington's main prop to protecting the low-wage export platform that Haiti had become. If the U.S. were to send in Marines, it wouldn't be so that a popular democracy could take root, but so that some sort of civilian cover for a 'regime serving U.S. interests could be installed. We don't know what the Haitian people are capable of doing on their own, but the last country in the world we should want to invite in to restore democracy in Haiti is that most consistent opponent of Haitian democracy, the U.S. government.

Moreover, having the U.S. intervene in Haiti (whether alone or at the head of some fig-leaf coalition) is problematic not just for Haitians, but for all those in the Third World who may later become victims of U.S. interventionism. Two years ago there was a great deal of discussion of the peace dividend and of closing down foreign military bases; today elements of the Left are drawing up missions for the Pentagon that will justify a bloated military budget and foreign bases for years to come.

In arguing for non-intervention, we often find ourselves aligned with isolationists, those who oppose foreign adventures not because of the harm the U.S. is likely to do, but because of the costs to the U.S. and a basic indifference to foreign suffering. We need to distinguish our views from those of both the isolationists and the interventionists.

When we hear Americans say "Don't send U.S. troops to Haiti, who cares about them," we need to reply: "Don't send U.S. troops to Haiti because we do care about the struggle of the Haitian people for justice and decent lives." When we hear others say, "Let's keep out of that Balkan quagmire where American lives will be lost in behalf of one crazy fanatic or another," we have to respond, "We support the Bosnian struggle for preserving a multi-ethnic state, and that's why we want NATO to stay out." Opposing U.S. intervention is not giving up on internationalism. It is almost always the best way to be an internationalist.

RECOGNIZING AUTHOR'S POINT OF VIEW

This activity may be used as an individualized study guide for students in libraries and resource centers or as a discussion catalyst in small group and classroom discussions.

The capacity to recognize an author's point of view is an essential reading skill. Many readers do not make clear distinctions between descriptive articles that relate factual information and articles that express a point of view. Think about the readings in Chapter Three. Are these readings essentially descriptive articles that relate factual information or articles that attempt to persuade through editorial commentary and analysis?

Guidelines

1. The following are possible descriptions of sources that appeared in Chapter Three. Choose one of the following descriptions that best defines each source in Chapter Three.

Source Descriptions

a. Essentially an article that relates factual information
b. Essentially an article that expresses editorial points of view
c. Both of the above
d. Neither of the above

Sources in Chapter Three

_____ *Source Eleven*
   "Preventing Global Genocide" by Jeane J.Kirkpatrick

_____ *Source Twelve*
"Say 'No' to Bosnian Intervention" by Harvey F. Egan

_____ *Source Thirteen*
"Intervention Must Come Early" by Carol Birkland

_____ *Source Fourteen*
"Pax Americana - Can Peace Be Imposed?" by Russel Kirk

_____ *Source Fifteen*
"When Military Intervention Is Necessary" by Lynne Jones

_____ *Source Sixteen*
"Military Intervention: Not for Me" by Stephen R. Shalom

2. Summarize the author's point of view in one to three sentences for each of the readings in Chapter Three.

3. After careful consderation, pick out one reading that you think is the most reliable source. Be prepared to explain the reasons for your choice in a general class discussion.

CHAPTER 4

MILITARISM AND THE ARMS TRADE

17 MILITARISM AND THE ARMS TRADE

THE NEED FOR MILITARY SUPREMACY

William R. Hawkins

William Hawkins is a senior research analyst for the Republican Research Committee.

Points to Consider:

1. Who is Anthony Lake and what is his perspective on the use of military intervention?

2. Describe current United States military strategy.

3. Why does the author believe our military capability is not adequate?

4. How do Army studies show a weakness in our nation's military strength?

William R. Hawkins, "Clinton Hollows vs. Military," **Human Events**, June 3, 1994. Reprinted with permission.

In any crisis, the first thing asked is, "Where are the carriers?" Yet the carrier force is being reduced both in the number of carriers (from 15 to 11 or 12) and in their capabilities.

National Security Adviser Anthony Lake in a lecture at Johns Hopkins University last fall said that "we should not oppose using our military forces for humanitarian purposes." Lake added that "Because the source of such threats will be diverse and unpredictable, we must seek to ensure that our forces are increasingly ready, mobile, flexible and smart..." Unfortunately, Bill Clinton's enthusiasm for military intervention is not matched by any concern for providing American troops with what they need to fight, win—and survive—in combat.

The precipitous down-sizing of American military forces has reduced available combat units to a level inadequate to fulfill the strategy set by President Bill Clinton. Current strategy calls for the capability to fight two nearly-simultaneous conflicts on the scale of the recent Persian Gulf War. Yet in the gulf war, the Army deployed eight divisions. The Army's current authorized force level is only 10 active divisions, down from 18 divisions active in 1989. In manpower this means cuts from the 790,000 Army troops available in 1989 to 510,000 in 1995 and 495,000 in 1997.

NO RESERVES AVAILABLE

The capability of the military to fight and win even one Persian Gulf-sized conflict is now in question. Forget about keeping in mind a cardinal principle of military thought: that having a reserve force available for other emergencies is essential.

Only five Army divisions are assigned to what is called Force Package 1, the "contingency corps" of divisions kept at full readiness for immediate commitment in time of crisis. Behind them are Force Package 2 (the forward-deployed units in Europe and South Korea); Force Package 3 (the remaining active divisions based in the United States); and Force Package 4 (National Guard and Reserve units).

ARMY STUDIES

Army studies show that, except for the contingency corps, the other packages are all declining in fighting skills as a result of cuts

111

Cartoon by Mike Ramirez. Reprinted with permission of **Copley News Service.**

that have reduced training and delayed or deferred maintenance and modernization programs. Package 2 "is losing its close combat edge." Package 3 "is not maintaining its land-force dominance" and Package 4 is "not maintaining its edge in any area."

For example, facilities-repair and maintenance funding has fallen by a third relative to the size of the force. Maintenance and supply per division have fallen by 22% and depot-maintenance per division has fallen by 38%. Hundreds fewer helicopter pilots are being trained than are needed. Last year, the Army in Europe had only 75% of its operations and maintenance requirements funded. As a result, tactical training was cut back 12% to cover the shortfall. It is from these ranks that Clinton would send troops to serve in Bosnia.

THE BUDGET

The Army is not the only service to suffer. Maintenance crews in the Air Force are struggling to keep on hand adequate numbers of jet engines for its first-line F-15 and F-16 fighters. Budget constraints have limited the purchase of spare parts and the service faces a 1,000-engine repair backlog. Though the Clinton Administration fiscal year (FY) 1995 budget request increases depot maintenance funding by $1.2 billion over FY 1994, this is still not enough to keep the backlog from increasing further in

1995.

Even those forces that can be expected to be the first into action
are seeing their capabilities degrade. Last fall, the head of the
U.S. Special Operations Command, Gen. Wayne Downing,
reported to the Pentagon that, due to defense budget cuts, he
would have to reduce operational readiness and training. He
would also have to cancel 42 programs and scale back 24 others.
Among the canceled programs was the MC-130H tanker upgrade.
Yet aerial refueling has become increasingly vital to the projection
of American forces overseas as units have been withdrawn from
forward-deployed bases and as the foreign bases themselves have
become inaccessible. Improvements in night vision and naviga-
tion equipment, essential for special operations, is also being
slowed.

In any crisis, the first thing asked is, "Where are the carriers?"
Yet the carrier force is being reduced both in the number of carriers (from 15 to 11 or 12) and in their capabilities. The Navy
reports serious shortfalls in two important procurement areas:
ship-building and aviation. In ship-building and the refueling of
the Navy's nuclear carriers, $1.2 billion is being allocated on
average during the years 1995-1999 when a $2-billion average is
needed to maintain planned levels. In aviation, the shortfall in the
F-18 program, the Navy's primary fighter-bomber, is about $900
million a year.

AIR POWER SUFFERS

Even such a hero of the Persian Gulf War as the F-117 "stealth fighter" is seeing its level of readiness fall. Inadequate logistics accounts have pushed its mission-capable rate below Air Force standards. Similar problems are also affecting the E-3 Airborne Warning and Control Systems aircraft and the F-15E and F-111 fighters. This is at a time when the swift commitment of airpower is being pushed as a substitute for the rapid deployment of a shrinking ground army.

Defense cuts have little to do with balancing the budget. During FY 1995-1999 the Congressional Budget Office forecasts deficits totalling $903 billion. Defense makes up only 18% of the budget, so defense cuts are neither the cause nor the cure for the chronic deficits. These cuts are imposing devastating reductions in military capabilities out of any proportion to the supposed fiscal benefit.

If trends are not reversed, the military will revert to the sad condition that scandalized the last Democratic President, Jimmy Carter in the 1970s. It will be a "hollow force" without the ability to sustain itself in combat even if it manages somehow to limp to the battlefield.

18   MILITARISM AND THE ARMS TRADE

EXCESSIVE MILITARY SPENDING

The Defense Monitor

The Center for Defense Information believes that strong social, economic, political, and military components and a healthy environment contribute equally to the nation's security. The Center opposes excessive expenditures for weapons that increase the danger of war.

Points to Consider:

1. Explain in detail the President's five-year plan for military spending.

2. How is domestic spending related to military spending?

3. Compare the military spending programs of the Bush and Clinton administrations.

4. Discuss the Aspen military plan known as Option C.

5. How does the author describe the costs of military spending?

6. Describe the needed changes in our global military spending and strategy.

"Excessive Military Spending," **The Defense Monitor**, Vol. 23, No. 5, 1994 and Vol. 22, No. 7, 1993.

Continued excessive military spending amounts to an immense waste of the nation's resources.

Although the United States faces no dangerous enemies, the Clinton Administration has decided to make only token reductions in Cold War levels of military spending. The rare opportunity for a large "peace dividend" afforded by the end of the Cold War is rapidly slipping away.

President Clinton has proposed raising the military budget from $261 billion in 1994 to $264 billion in 1995. The budget differs from the actual spending shown elsewhere in this *Defense Monitor* because money is not always spent in the year it is budgeted. Money leftover from previous years will raise actual 1995 spending above the 1995 budget to an estimated $271 billion.

The President's 5-year plan for military spending will quickly consume $1.3 trillion. That's $1,300,000,000,000. To print all that money at a rate of $1,000 per minute would take over 24 centuries! The President has argued that major domestic problems such as poverty, education, crime, and pollution urgently need attention. Reducing unnecessary military spending may be one of the only ways to provide funds to address these problems in a time of continuing scarce government resources.

CLINTON ADMINISTRATION'S MILITARY SPENDING PLAN

Billions of Dollars

1995	1996	1997	1998	1999	1995-99
271	261	256	257	258	1,302

Congressional legislation has put caps on certain spending categories. Domestic programs now must compete for funds out of the same pot of money as the military. If military spending plans are increased, as the Clinton Administration has done, it means domestic programs will receive that much less money...

The onset of a new administration holds the promise of change. But after 45 years of the Cold War, we must be careful that we make changes for the better. The Pentagon, driven by a desire to maintain huge budgets and armed forces, is preparing for change by increasing its ability to intervene around the world. Is this change for the better?

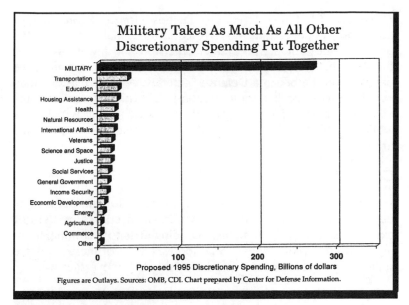

Military Takes As Much As All Other
Discretionary Spending Put Together

MILITARY	
Transportation	
Education	
Housing Assistance	
Health	
Natural Resources	
International Affairs	
Veterans	
Science and Space	
Justice	
Social Services	
General Government	
Income Security	
Economic Development	
Energy	
Agriculture	
Commerce	
Other	

0   100   200   300
Proposed 1995 Discretionary Spending, Billions of dollars

Figures are Outlays. Sources: OMB, CDI. Chart prepared by Center for Defense Information.

Center for Defense Information.

The United States is the only nation in the world which maintains large, costly armed forces solely for intervention in the affairs of foreign nations. As Secretary of Defense Les Aspin said, "This is what really determines the size of the defense budget now...It is essentially defense budgets that are built around being able to handle regional threats."

The Pentagon acknowledges that the end of the Cold War allows it to reduce the size of our armed forces. Yet the Pentagon still asserts that uncertainty in the world dictates that the United States prepare for a wide variety of new "threats" with this huge force...

MORE OF THE SAME

Thus far the Clinton Administration does not differ greatly from the Bush Administration in its approach to funding the Pentagon or in intervening around the world. During his election campaign Clinton proposed a 5-year military budget (Fiscal Years 1993-97) of $1.36 trillion, $60 billion less than President Bush, a difference of only 4 percent. In a campaign speech he said, "We need to develop greater air and sea lift capacity, including production of the C-17 transport aircraft."

President Clinton's Secretary of Defense, former Representative Les Aspin, believes that modern technology makes possible the use of military force with greater precision and fewer casualties, thus making going to war more politically acceptable than in the past. Before he became Defense Secretary, Aspin released a plan which came to be known as "Option C." This plan calls for the U.S. to be able to fight the equivalent of another war with Iraq as well as two other lesser regional contingencies, all at the same time.

COSTS OF INTERVENTION

Maintaining large standing forces, largely for the purpose of being able to fight around the world is, of course, extremely expensive. The bulk of military spending goes to recruiting, training, and equipping conventional forces. Most of these units are stationed overseas or considered available for an overseas war.

As the Pentagon restructures, it is reorganizing its units into four so-called "force packages." These are the Strategic, Contingency, Atlantic, and Pacific forces. Strategic forces include all long-range nuclear weapons. The latter two are dedicated to Europe/Middle East and East Asia respectively. Contingency forces would provide the initial forces for rapid deployment overseas, including some of the nation's premier intervention forces such as the Army's 82nd Airborne and 101st Air Mobile divisions and a Marine Expeditionary Force.

These planned interventionary forces will include 12 active and 6 reserve Army divisions, 16 active and 11 reserve tactical fighter wings, 12 carrier battle groups, 3 Marine Expeditionary Forces, and 3 Amphibious Ready Groups. The total annual cost for these forces, including unallocated combat and support units, will be $195 billion in FY 1993 dollars...

NEEDED CHANGES

Since President Clinton took office, he has been told that he must turn his attention to so-called vital foreign policy and military issues. But that advice usually comes with the warning that he must not make deep cuts in Pentagon budgets and forces.

The truth today is that there is no serious military challenge to the United States anywhere in the world. It is by now a truism, but worth repeating, that in the aftermath of the Cold War, the

United States has the most powerful military establishment, far stronger than any other country or group of countries, and faces no active or foreseeable threat to its security. Yet despite this fact, the Pentagon still plans to devote $195 billion a year to train and equip its forces to intervene around the world, primarily in developing nations.

Calls to preserve huge U.S. military spending have no validity. They represent the resistance of the deeply entrenched military-industrial special interests who cannot imagine a different way of doing things. If military spending goes on at Cold War levels for "expeditionary forces" and "Special Forces" designed to "project American power" into regional conflicts, U.S. leaders will have to demonstrate that the money has been spent wisely. There will be tremendous pressure to rely on our military strength to deal with global problems that have no military solution. We will find ourselves always at war, or on the brink of war, in distant regions of the world, using our military forces for purposes having nothing to do with the legitimate defense of the United States.

President Clinton has proposed some limited cuts in the Pentagon. These are good first steps, but he can go much further. In fact, the United States can more than adequately defend itself as well as carry out all legitimate overseas tasks with far lower spending and forces. According to CDI's analysis, this can be accomplished with military spending of $200 billion a year and one million active and one million reserve forces (See *Defense Monitor* Vol. XXI, No. 4).

What is required is the recognition that future world leadership by the U.S. will be based not on military superiority but on American political, economic, and social institutions. Spending only marginally less for a vast military establishment will not come to grips with the underlying reality that we no longer need a huge Cold War establishment. When Bill Clinton was elected to office, it was an affirmation of his call for change. He should be encouraged to include the Pentagon in that mandate.

19   MILITARISM AND THE ARMS TRADE

PREPARING FOR MILITARY INTERVENTION IN A DANGEROUS WORLD

The U.S. Department of Defense

The following comments were excerpted from the Bottom Up Review, *a Defense Department Report headed by Les Aspin, President Clinton's first Secretary of Defense. This report is a comprehensive review of the nation's defense strategy, force structure, modernization, infrastructure, and foundations.*

Points to Consider:

1. List and explain the new dangers the United States faces in the post-Cold War era.

2. Name the two types of nuclear weapons that are continuing to grow. List the five declared nuclear weapon states.

3. What role must the United States play in the post-Cold War era?

4. Describe regional dangers, and how they relate to United States security.

5. Why is it important for the United States to maintain sufficient power with regard to regional conflicts?

6. What are some of the benefits to stationing United States forces abroad?

Excerpted from "Report on the *Bottom Up Review,*" U.S. Department of Defense, 1993.

By stationing forces abroad we also improve our ability to respond effectively to crises or aggression when they occur.

The Cold War is behind us. The Soviet Union is no longer. The threat that drove our defense decision-making for four and a half decades—that determined our strategy and tactics, our doctrine, the size and shape of our forces, the designs of our weapons, and the size of our defense budgets—is gone.

Now that the Cold War is over, the questions we face in the Department of Defense are: How do we structure the armed forces of the United States for the future? How much defense is enough in the post-Cold War Era?

AN ERA OF NEW DANGERS

Most striking in the transition from the Cold War is the shift in the nature of the dangers to our interests. The new dangers fall into four broad categories:

- *Dangers posed by nuclear weapons and other weapons of mass destruction,* including dangers associated with the proliferation of nuclear, biological, and chemical weapons as well as those associated with the large stocks of these weapons that remain in the former Soviet Union.

- *Regional dangers,* posed primarily by the threat of large-scale aggression by major regional powers with interests antithetical to our own, but also by the potential for smaller, often internal, conflicts based on ethnic or religious animosities, state-sponsored terrorism, or subversion of friendly governments.

- *Dangers to democracy and reform,* in the former Soviet Union, Eastern Europe, and elsewhere.

- *Economic dangers* to our national security, which could result if we fail to build a strong, competitive and growing economy.

Our armed forces are central to combating the first two dangers and can play a significant role in meeting the second two. Our predictions and conclusions about the nature and characteristics of these dangers will help mold our strategy and size, and shape our future military forces.

121

New Dangers

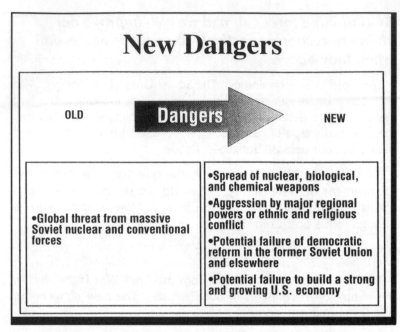

OLD   **Dangers**   NEW

•Global threat from massive Soviet nuclear and conventional forces	•Spread of nuclear, biological, and chemical weapons •Aggression by major regional powers or ethnic and religious conflict •Potential failure of democratic reform in the former Soviet Union and elsewhere •Potential failure to build a strong and growing U.S. economy

U.S. Department of Defense.

Dangers posed by nuclear weapons and other weapons of mass destruction (WMD)—that is, biological and chemical weapons—are growing. Beyond the five declared nuclear-weapon states (the United States, Russia, France, Great Britain, and China), at least 20 other nations either have acquired or are attempting to acquire weapons of mass destruction.

In addition to cooperative threat reduction and nonproliferation efforts, the United States will need to retain the capacity for nuclear retaliation against those who might contemplate the use of weapons of mass destruction. We must also continue to explore other ways to improve our ability to counter proliferation, such as active and passive defenses against nuclear, biological, and chemical weapons and their delivery systems.

REGIONAL DANGERS AND OPPORTUNITIES

Regional dangers include a host of threats: large-scale aggression; smaller conflicts; internal strife caused by ethnic, tribal, or religious animosities; state-sponsored terrorism; subversion of friendly governments; insurgencies; and drug trafficking. Each of these dangers jeopardizes, to varying degrees, interests important to the United States.

Beyond these dangers, there are also real opportunities. During the Cold War, repressive regimes that were direct adversaries of the United States dominated vast regions of the globe. Today, the countries that pose direct dangers to us are far fewer, and the countries that may join us in thwarting the remaining regional dangers are far more numerous.

ADDRESSING REGIONAL DANGERS AND SEIZING OPPORTUNITIES

To address the new regional dangers and seize new opportunities, we have developed a multifaceted strategy based on defeating aggressors in major regional conflicts, maintaining overseas presence to deter conflicts and provide regional stability, and conducting smaller-scale intervention operations, such as peace enforcement, peacekeeping, humanitarian assistance, and disaster relief to further U.S. interests and objectives.

Major Regional Conflicts. The United States will continue to have important interests and allies in many regions of the world, from Europe through Southwest Asia, into East Asia, and elsewhere. Regional aggressors represent a danger that must be deterred and, if necessary, defeated by the military capability of the United States and its allies. Moreover, if we were to be drawn into a war in response to the armed aggression of one hostile nation, another could well be tempted to attack its neighbors— especially if it were convinced the United States and its allies did not possess the requisite military capability or will to oppose it.

Therefore, it is prudent for the United States to maintain sufficient military power to be able to win two major regional conflicts

123

that occur nearly simultaneously. With this capability, we will be confident, and our allies as well as potential enemies will know, that a single regional conflict will not leave our interests and allies in other regions at risk.

Further, sizing our forces for two major regional conflicts provides a hedge against the possibility that a future adversary might one day confront us with a larger-than-expected threat, and then turn out, through doctrinal or technological innovation, to be more capable than we expect, or enlist the assistance of other nations to form a coalition against our interests. The dynamic and unpredictable post-Cold War environment demands that we maintain military capabilities flexible and responsive enough to cope with unforeseen dangers. Thus, U.S. forces will be structured to achieve decisive victory in two nearly simultaneous major regional conflicts and to conduct combat operations characterized by rapid response and a high probability of success, while minimizing the risk of significant American casualties.

Overseas Presence. Stationing and deploying U.S. military forces overseas in peacetime is an essential element in dealing with new regional dangers and pursuing new opportunities.

The peacetime overseas presence of our forces is the single most visible demonstration of our commitment to defend U.S. and allied interests in Europe, Asia, and elsewhere around the world. The presence of U.S. forces deters adventurism and coercion by potentially hostile states, reassures friends, enhances regional stability, and underwrites our larger strategy of international engagement, prevention, and partnership. It also gives us a stronger influence, both political and economic as well as military, in the affairs of key regions.

Our overseas presence provides the leading edge of the rapid response capability that we would need in a crisis. Moreover, our day-to-day operations with allies improve the ability of U.S. and allied forces to operate effectively together.

Finally, our routine presence helps to ensure our access to the facilities and bases we would need during a conflict or contingency, both to operate in a given region and to deploy forces from the United States to distant regions.

Peacekeeping, Peace Enforcement, and Other Intervention Operations. While deterring and defeating major regional aggression will be the most demanding requirement of the new defense strategy, our emphasis on engagement, prevention, and partnership means that, in this new era, U.S. military forces are more likely to be involved in operations short of declared or intense warfare. Events of the past few years have already borne this out, as our armed forces have been involved in a wide range of so-called "intervention" operations, from aiding typhoon victims in Bangladesh during Operation Sea Angel, to delivering humanitarian relief to the former Soviet Union under Operation Provide Hope, to conducting the emergency evacuation of U.S. citizens from Liberia during Operation Sharp Edge, to restoring order and aiding the victims of the civil war in Somalia during Operation Restore Hope.

Through overseas presence and power projection, our armed forces can help deter or contain violence in volatile regions where our interests are threatened. In some circumstances, U.S. forces can serve a peacekeeping role, monitoring and facilitating the implementation of cease-fire and peace agreements with the consent of the belligerent parties as part of a U.N. or other coalition presence. In more hostile situations, the United States might be called upon, along with other nations, to provide forces to compel compliance with international resolutions or to restore order in peace enforcement operations. In some cases, such as Operation Just Cause in Panama, we may intervene unilaterally to protect our interests. Finally, our armed forces will continue to play an important role in the national effort to halt the importation of illegal drugs to the United States.

In the future, there are likely to be many occasions when we are asked to intervene with military force overseas. In deciding where, when, and how our military should be employed for peace enforcement, peacekeeping, humanitarian relief, or similar types of operations, we will need to consider each situation individually and carefully weigh many factors.

20 MILITARISM AND THE ARMS TRADE

THE UNITED STATES AS
WORLD SUPERCOP

Eugene J. Carroll

*Eugene J. Carroll is a retired Navy Rear Admiral. He is the direc-
tor of the Center for Defense Information in Washington, D.C.*

Points to Consider:

1. How has military force been used in United States history?

2. How can the United States avoid playing the role of the
   world's policeman?

3. What costs are associated with military operations?

4. What problems have occurred in the United States due to
   excessive military spending?

5. List and explain the three options the United States has with
   regard to peacekeeping.

Eugene J. Carroll, "Policing World Trouble Spots," **The Defense Monitor**, Vol. 23,
No. 3, 1994.

Drugs, crime, violence, and broken families mix with poverty in an explosive domestic witches' brew. Nearly half of American adults are functionally illiterate. More than 37 million Americans lack any form of health care.

The United States has a long history of using armed force. World Wars I and II were its biggest conflicts, but the U.S. has been involved in many other wars. The U.S. attacked Native Americans and Mexico during its westward expansion, became a colonial power after its victory in the Spanish-American War, and occupied Central American and Caribbean countries during the early 20th Century.

The Cold War gave a fresh impetus to U.S. military interventions. In the name of anticommunism, U.S. forces intervened unilaterally in Lebanon (1958), the Dominican Republic (1965), Vietnam, Laos, Cambodia (1965-73), and Grenada (1983). The United States invaded Panama (1989) and used the United Nations as a cover for essentially American military operations in Korea (1950-53) and Iraq (1991). Proxy armies at the Bay of Pigs in Cuba and the Contras in Nicaragua, plus so-called covert operations to overthrow foreign governments in Iran, Guatemala, and Chile substituted for the direct use of U.S. armed forces.

WORLD'S POLICEMAN

For 40 years, the United States played the role of the world's policeman against the Soviet Union. The Cold War was the era of two big rival military powers. Now, there's just the United States. Current U.S. military plans suggest that the policeman's role is still intact under a new guise. The Pentagon's 1993 "Bottom-Up Review" concluded that the U.S. needed military forces structured to fight and win two "major regional conflicts" (comparable to the war with Iraq) almost simultaneously and without allies. American equipment and forces continue to be stationed around the world, ready to intervene immediately anywhere, anytime U.S. interests are deemed to be in jeopardy.

If the United States, now the strongest military and economic power in the world, is to shift away from the self-appointed mission of global cop, it must first consider practical alternative approaches to the unilateral use of force. One possibility is for the U.S. to share the job of peacekeeping around the world more

127

Cartoon by Mike Keefe.

equally with the other members of the United Nations...

In 1992 the United States spent $2,016 on its own military for each dollar it spent on U.N. peacekeeping. Today, the U.S. Congress is dragging its feet on contributions to U.N. peacekeeping while continuing to fund the U.S. military at Cold War levels. Congress has expressed its displeasure with U.N. operations by cutting funding requests for U.N peacekeeping during 1994. Meanwhile, the Defense Department wants an additional $20 billion above the amount already budgeted for military purposes during the next 5 years...

BOUTROS-GHALI'S PROPOSALS

Prevention

Clinton's current approach also differs markedly from the one advanced by U.N. Secretary General Boutros Boutros-Ghali. In his 1992 report, *An Agenda for Peace*, Boutros-Ghali emphasized both "preventive diplomacy" and more permanent arrangements for the possible use of armed force. Preventive diplomacy is intended to avoid a crisis. It could include: fact-finding missions; early warning systems concerning natural disasters, nuclear accidents, and the threat of famine; and the establishment of demilitarized zones. If diplomacy proves inadequate and a threatened country requests it, Boutros-Ghali recommends the preventive deployment of a U.N. force along international borders in order to ward off potential invaders.

If Kuwait had requested U.N. troops along its border with Iraq early in 1990, might not Saddam Hussein have thought twice before attacking? And what would have happened if street-smart community organizers, trained in listening to people's grievances and backed by interpreters, had accompanied the first U.N. peacekeepers into Mogadishu, the capital of Somalia? We can't know the answers, but they raise intriguing possibilities for more effective use of U.N. military strength in the future.

The Secretary General's proposals for the use of armed force by the U.N. recall the design envisaged by the founders of the world body. Under Article 43 of the U.N. Charter, member nations were expected to negotiate agreements with the Security Council which designated units of their armed forces to be on stand-by for use in emergencies. Because of the Cold War, no agreements were reached...

Three Paths

The United States has three options with regard to peacekeeping. **First**, the U.S. can ignore the U.N. and continue to act as world policeman, with regional conflicts replacing communist expansion as the perceived danger. This approach legitimizes Cold War military spending levels to fund massive, highly mobile, combat-ready armed forces deployed worldwide at foreign bases and in powerful naval fleets. This approach virtually assures continued U.S. involvement in conflicts around the world for the foreseeable future. Moreover, the present levels of military spending to support the world policeman role will undermine our ability to meet pressing domestic needs at home.

Second, the U.S. can act as world policeman, as it has in the past, while using the U.N. as a cover for military action. During the Korean War, the U.N. General Headquarters and the U.S. Far East Command Headquarters were, in reality, one and the same. Even this fiction was abandoned in the Gulf War, although President Bush attempted to cloak U.S. operations under a series of "authorizing" U.N. resolutions.

In the future, the United States could continue to follow the Gulf War pattern by seeking resolutions of U.N. support from the

Security Council while exercising U.S. command of predominantly American forces. This approach could involve more countries in military actions and marginally reduce costs to the Pentagon, but it would only be a facade, masking basically unilateral U.S. actions.

Third, the U.S. can become a major leader in building a more effective United Nations. This would require not only political, financial, and military support for U.N. peacekeeping, but also a determination to work closely with other countries in building new structures for international security. This approach could lead within a few years to more equal burden-sharing in meeting potential threats to the peace, lower levels of military spending throughout the world, and an increase in resources available to address acute domestic problems. If the U.N. is to achieve these objectives, it is imperative that the U.S. take the lead in fostering U.N. organizational reform and contribute its own military, political, and administrative expertise.

A TOUGHER FIGHT AT HOME

Worldwide military spending in 1992 totaled about $742 billion. U.S. military spending accounted for roughly 40% of this amount. The United States has emerged from the Cold War with a formidable backlog of problems at home that urgently demand public attention. One in seven Americans lives below the poverty line. By helping to build a more effective United Nations, the United States could wind down its role as world policeman and begin at last to address the violence on its cities' streets, the gaps in its schools' educational programs, the decay of its infrastructure, the pollution of its air, soil, and water, and the need for good jobs in new industries. Until we bring our global military commitments into better balance with pressing national needs at home, the security and well-being of all Americans will suffer.

130

21 MILITARISM AND THE ARMS TRADE

PROMOTING PEACE AND SECURITY

Anna Stout

Anna Stout is the Executive Vice President of the American League for Exports and Security Assistance.

Points to Consider:

1. Why is it in the interest of the United States to export arms overseas?

2. Explain how arms sales can play a positive role in the world.

3. Explain the new threats to the United States national security.

Excerpted from Congressional testimony by Anna Stout before the House Committee on Foreign Affairs, November 9, 1993.

131

Consider the role played by U.S. arms sales in strengthening the Atlantic alliance in our collective effort to contain and secure victory in the Cold War.

I have been dealing for a considerable period with the issue of arms sales, both in government and in private industry. My experience has shown me that it has been and continues to be in the U.S. national interest to have an arms export policy that allows friends and Allies to acquire American-made defense articles and services. The sale of arms, at its core, is the "currency" of diplomacy. By that I mean, the transfer of arms by one country to another represents one of the most fundamental transactions between nations.

It connotes a high level of trust, solidarity and a coincidence of the most elemental concern between two nations, that of self-defense. And when those transfers occur between the U.S. and those nations allied with our goals and interests, the cause of liberty is strengthened.

COLLECTIVE EFFORTS

Consider the role played by U.S. arms sales in strengthening the Atlantic alliance in our collective effort to contain and ultimately secure victory in the Cold War. Italians and then-West Germans flew American made F-100s, F-104s and F-4 Phantoms. Greek and Turkish tank crews operated U.S. M-41s, M-47s and M-60s. Our cooperation with our Allies served notice to potential enemies of our willingness to defend one another. Deterrence was strengthened.

The ability of the U.S. to share with our allies the means to defend themselves, at a time when they were incapable of doing so independently, was a critical determinant in our collective effort to contain the Soviet threat.

Another example of the positive role played by a constructive arms sales policy is that of the Camp David Peace Accords signed between the governments of Egypt and Israel. That agreement was, in large part, cemented by a U.S. commitment to provide tens of billions of dollars in military assistance to the two signatories. Security assistance was used, in this case, to bind the peace that had been agreed upon and to ensure that both parties were confident of their respective ability to defend themselves, to be their own guarantors. What progress has been made to date in building upon the Camp David Peace Accords owes much to the U.S. security assistance provided to Egypt and Israel.

THE NEW WORLD

Today, the specter of Soviet aggression is gone. People in some quarters correctly question whether the rationale underlying our fundamental arms sales policy has also disappeared. I wish only that all active and latent threats to our security and that of our Allies disappeared along with the Soviet Union. Even a cursory assessment shows that threats to our security and that of our friends, Allies and interests remain.

It is readily apparent that what we considered to be secondary and tertiary threats around the world during the Cold War, and often viewed through a Cold War lens, have, if anything, exploded to the forefront. Long simmering territorial, cultural and economic disputes have risen and are rising from long periods of dormancy made possible by the Cold War.

These threats to our national security remain real so long as our national interest continues to be defined, in part, by the security of our friends, Allies and interests that often are far from our borders. And because this definition of national interest is likely to be accepted for the foreseeable future, our nation will continue to be called upon to provide security assistance to peoples and governments whose aspirations coincide with our own.

President Clinton has told reporters that he wishes he could lift the arms embargo on the embattled Bosnian government locked in a struggle for its very survival in the enclave of the former Capital City of Sarajevo. In very real ways, arms sales and other forms of security assistance are understood by government officials to be critical tools in our nation's ability to stave off the advances of those bent on goals inimical to our interests and to help our friends and Allies secure and maintain the peace.

JUSTIFYING ARMS SALES

There are those who maintain that all arms sales are bad and that the United States should set an example for all other nations to follow by no longer selling defense articles and defense services to Allies and friends. I disagree. Let me explain why.

An arms sale does not take place in a vacuum. Every sale is surrounded by circumstances and related issues. For example, our

ARMS SALES DECLINE

Overall arms transfers to the Third World are declining dramatically, whether measured in terms of actual deliveries or new agreements. When measured in terms of actual deliveries, conventional arms transfers have declined steadily since 1987, when they were valued at well over $50 billion. This compares to calendar 1992, when deliveries were estimated at about $13 billion.

Furthermore, I believe that the current U.S. arms transfer process works not only well, but extremely well. Overall, U.S. sales are not destabilizing in nature: they respond to legitimate defense requirements; they are subject to careful review both within the administration and the Congress.

From Congressional testimony by William B. Inglee, former Deputy Assistant Secretary of Defense for conventional forces and arms control policy, November 9, 1993.

longstanding defense cooperative ties with England are deservedly well-supported throughout government. Our arms sales policy with respect to England is inextricable from the larger, historical "special relationship" our two countries enjoy.

The question needs to be put to those who generally oppose arms sales: Should we stop selling arms to Britain? Israel? And what of Norway or South Korea? Japan? Does anyone believe we should refrain from transferring armored personnel carriers, helmets or radios to troops serving under the command of the United Nations in Bosnia, Macedonia, Cambodia or Somalia? I think we can all agree that sales to those countries and institutions—sales that support the security of those nations and our common defense—are in our national interest and serve to advance those principles we hold in high esteem and that those sales should be continued.

ENDING ARMS SALES

I would argue that the broad debate is not really about whether the U.S. should provide arms, but to whom should we make arms available and under what circumstances. It is hard not to notice that some who charge, "Stop all U.S. arms sales," in truth have in mind other aims. Those who say they oppose arms sales in general should be specific. Stop which sales? To which countries should we stop selling defense equipment and services?

Most often such opposition to specific sales is from opponents who are really arguing that specific countries are not worthy of buying or receiving U.S. defense equipment. Opponents of specific sales should not hide behind generalities, but should address the root of their opposition.

The world is still in the midst of adjusting to the ongoing, fundamental change moving through the global security environment. The dramatic lessening of tensions made possible by the successful conclusion of the Cold War has led to an overall decline in defense budgets. Government procurement of defense systems and services has also largely declined across the globe.

The Pacific Rim is the only exception. Flush with the fruits of far-reaching economic expansion, nations within Asia now have the means to acquire very capable military systems to defend their rapidly growing interests. The evolving political and military situation there, largely spurred by the disappearance of the Soviet Union, is far from having defined itself. The state of flux is the most distinguished characteristic in this region. Until such time as the region is able to settle into a more profound security, Asian countries will continue to invest against instability by obtaining more capable defense forces.

THE NATIONAL INTEREST

Of course, I am not advocating we pursue sales that are not in our national interest. I do not know of anyone who is. If we can agree that a particular sale of U.S. equipment would advance our national interest, then we should go all out to win that contract.

I would suggest that the world market for defense sales is a finite one. Only so many defense industrial bases can be sustained by the current level of world-wide defense procurements and R&D. If we do not make those legitimate overseas sales, we lose economic and national security advantages that will only too willingly be picked up by others to our ultimate disadvantage.

22   MILITARISM AND THE ARMS TRADE

ARMING A VIOLENT WORLD

The Friends Committee on National Legislation

The Friends Committee on National Legislation (FCNL) includes Friends appointed by 26 Friends Yearly Meetings and by eight other Friends' organizations in the United States. Expressions of views in the FCNL Washington Newsletter *are guided by the Statement of Policy, prepared and approved by the Committee. Seeking to follow the ideas of the Spirit, the FCNL speaks for itself and for like-minded Friends.*

Points to Consider:

1. What countries dominate the arms trade? Why does the FCNL oppose the arms trade?

2. According to United States arms dealers, what good is achieved through arms sales?

3. What are arms transfers, and how do they happen?

4. What is FCNL's suggested policy to deal with the issue of the arms trade?

5. Who is working in Washington to promote change in the United States policy on the arms trade?

6. What can Americans do to stop the arms trade?

"What's Wrong with the Arms Trade?" **Friends Committee on National Legislation Washington Newsletter**, July 1993.

Since the end of the cold war, the U.S. has emerged as a leading arms merchant.

In the developing world, conventional weapons transfers drive conflicts into a spiraling cycle of armed violence, fomenting regional arms races and diverting scarce resources toward military buildup and away from development and commercial trade. Since 1945, while attention was focused on the threat of U.S.-Soviet nuclear confrontation, conventional weapons transfers to the developing world fueled regional wars that are estimated to have led to the deaths of 40 million people.

Between October 1, 1991, and September 30, 1992, the U.S. government entered into contracts worth over $16 billion in foreign military sales to more than 90 countries. Sixty-four percent of these sales were to the developing world, primarily to the Middle East. During the same period, another $16 billion in commercial sales to more than 144 countries were licensed by the U.S. government. Foreign military sales for fiscal year 1993 are estimated to be as high as $26.4 billion.

The U.S. is not the only government that is selling. Although the U.S. dominates, other suppliers—France, Russia, United Kingdom, China, and Germany—are actively working to hold on to their portions in the market. In January and February 1993, for instance, while the U.S. was making a deal to sell M1A2 tanks to Kuwait, France and the U.K. also contracted major sales to the Middle East. Corporate competition for arms markets drives government policies away from cooperation for multilateral arms restraint among the major suppliers.

WHAT DO U.S. MILITARY INDUSTRIES WANT?

U.S. arms dealers assert that good purposes are achieved by the transfer of U.S. weapons. They argue that arms sales promote national self-defense for U.S. allies and provide deterrence which prevents the outbreak of wars. They also claim that these sales increase U.S. influence in other regions of the world and seal alliances with foreign governments. In their view, the arms trade actually helps make the world safer.

In our view, though, their main argument for weapons transfers is the domestic economy—jobs. With the Pentagon buying less, these industries are putting tremendous pressure on legislators and the administration to support overseas sales as a way to keep pro-

" YES, (50 MILLION, 60 MILLION) SADDAM HUSSEIN (70 MILLION, 80 MILLION) IS
A TYRANT THAT (90 MILLION, 100 MILLION) MUST BE STOPPED.... "

Reprinted with permission of **The Milwaukee Journal.**

duction lines open. Promoting arms exports is touted as an alternative to economic transition from military to civilian production. Basically, arms dealers would "rather fight than switch." Motivated by profit, they ignore the very real consequences of their short-sighted and dangerous practices.

WHAT ARE "ARMS TRANSFERS" AND HOW DO THEY HAPPEN?

The term "conventional arms transfer" describes the exchange of non-nuclear, non-chemical, or non-biological military equipment, weapons systems, or technology by grant, cash or credit. Most weapons transfers are made between governments, and are known as foreign military sales. Commercial sales, or transactions between private weapons industries and governments, are becoming more prevalent.

The Arms Export Control Act (AECA) governs both types of sales. When a foreign government wants to buy U.S. military equipment it has seen advertised or actually used in combat, it contacts the U.S. government, usually the Departments of Defense and State. If the U.S. and the interested buyer decide to initiate a sale, the Departments of State and Defense will generate the necessary documentation, depending on the specific transaction. The sale will then go forward if Congress does not act to oppose it.

Under AECA, Congress can block sales that exceed a set monetary figure, depending on the type of service or equipment to be transferred. If Congress wishes to oppose the sale, both House and Senate must pass joint resolutions stating that intent. These resolutions will then be forwarded to the President. However, even if Congress does pass these resolutions, the sale is still likely to go through because the President may exercise the veto. As with any other bill, a veto can be overturned only by a two-thirds vote in both houses.

WHAT ARE FCNL'S PREFERRED POLICY OBJECTIVES?

FCNL opposes weapons transfers, from any country to any country. Comprehensive economic conversion projects, to help defense-dependent industries and communities change to a civilian industrial base, offer a sound alternative to the policy of promoting arms exports.

Multilateral peace processes, demilitarizing international conflicts, eliminating military aid from U.S. foreign aid programs, and putting scarce resources toward development in the Third World (and not toward arms races) can replace the current global security systems that are based on a so-called military balance of power.

WHO IN WASHINGTON IS WORKING TO REVERSE U.S. ARMS TRANSFERS POLICY?

FCNL currently facilitates a Washington-based group of 45 national organizations representing religious, scientific, human rights, peace, women's and arms control communities. It is known as the Arms Trade Working Group (ATWG). ATWG seeks to promote changes in U.S. policy that will make the problem of conventional weapons transfers more visible to the public and make the system more accountable. Specific steps ATWG has identified that would promote those goals include:

• Holding full-scale hearings on U.S. arms export policy in the Foreign Affairs/Foreign Relations Committees.

SUBSIDY FOR WAR

Arms sales fuel regional arms races that in turn are used to justify additional Pentagon spending for "regional contingencies," costing taxpayers tens of billions of dollars in added military budget costs every year. And last but not least, pushing arms on Third-World countries stunts their economic growth, reducing demand for other goods and services in the process.

William D. Hartung, "Sale of the Century," **Commonweal**, May 20, 1994.

- Extending the land mines moratorium and fostering U.S. leadership for an international ban on land mines.

- Increasing access to information by requiring that all sales, once announced, be entered into the Congressional Record. Also, enforce an AECA provision requiring that the list of projected sales for the year (known as the Javits List) be declassified and available to the public.

HOW CAN YOU HELP?

Recognizing that U.S. weapons are being sold today to tomorrow's "hot spots," grassroots groups have formed in several major cities... If you want to be active in halting the arms trade, contact FCNL; we may be able to put you in touch with like-minded folks in your area.

EXAMINING COUNTERPOINTS

This activity may be used as an individualized study guide for students in libraries and resource centers or as a discussion catalyst in small group and classroom discussions.

The Point
Exclusive war powers rest with the President.
The Counterpoint
Exclusive war powers rest with the Congress.

• • •

The Point
Military intervention by the United Nations is necessary in genocides like Bosnia and Rwanda.
The Counterpoint
The United Nations should not intervene militarily in internal or civil wars.

• • •

The Point
The global arms trade should be abolished.
The Counterpoint
The global arms trade is necessary in a dangerous world.

Guidelines

Examine the counterpoints above and then consider the following questions.

1. Do you agree more with the point or counterpoint in each case? Why?

2. Which reading in this publication best illustrates the point in each case?

3. Which reading best illustrates each counterpoint?

4. Summarize the meaning of the cartoon below.

Cartoon by Carol & Simpson.

CHAPTER 5

THE UNITED NATIONS & WORLD ORDER

23   THE UNITED NATIONS & WORLD ORDER

PEACE KEEPING THROUGH THE UNITED NATIONS

United Nations Association of the U.S.A.

The United Nations Association of the United States of America is a private non-profit association that promotes understanding of the history and current activities of the United Nations throughout the world.

Points to Consider:

1. Why would the United Nations Security Council and Military Staff need to be reformed for effective United Nations military action?

2. Discuss the seven responsibilities the Military Staff Committee needs to undertake in order to play the role originally envisioned for it under the United Nations charter.

3. List and explain the "multi-tiered system" proposed for United Nations military action.

4. What is needed to accomplish the "multi-tiered system?"

Excerpted from a statement by the United Nations Association of the United States of America before the House Committee on Government Operations, March 3, 1994.

U.N. military capability needs to be strong enough to provide an effective deterrent to would-be aggressors.

The evolving Russian-American strategic relationship promises new possibilities for cooperation in international peacekeeping, peacemaking, and peace enforcement. To deal with conflicts as diverse as Somalia, Bosnia, and the Persian Gulf, however, the international community will need a varied and highly flexible arsenal of conflict-resolution, nation-building, and military-enforcement capabilities. A series of steps will need to be taken, in particular, if the United Nations is to be in a position to carry out the very serious business of military enforcement.

The Security Council should be selective in deciding when and where to intervene militarily. When the Council decides to undertake an enforcement operation, it should do so with sufficient application of force to be assured of a positive outcome. In this context, it would be counterproductive for the U.N. to establish a standing or permanent supra-national force because it is the direct involvement and commitment of the major military powers that provide the military muscle and the political credibility for a multilateral enforcement action. This linkage must be maintained if lives are not to be risked needlessly.

U.N. military capability needs to be strong enough and credible enough to provide an effective deterrent to would-be aggressors and adaptable enough to be employed in a wide range of contingencies. In this regard the United States and Russia should support U.N. military operations as one of the official missions of their armed forces. As called for by Article 43 of the U.N. Charter, they should indicate to the Council what forces they are willing to make available, and undertake to have these forces prepared for international duty through joint training and exercises with stand-by forces from other U.N. member states. The commitment of these forces for specific missions should not be automatic, but instead should be conditioned on the approval of the constitutional processes of the member state.

REFORM

The Security Council and the Military Staff Committee need to be reformed and restructured if the U.N. is to conduct military enforcement successfully. To bolster its political credibility, the Security Council should be made more representative of the entire

PLACES THAT COULD USE A GOOD DOUSING

Cartoon by Joe Heller.

U.N. membership, while remaining small enough for effective decision-making. The Security Council also needs the best professional military input it can get. Consequently, the Military Staff Committee should be allowed to play the role originally envisioned for it in the U.N. Charter. By building an extensive staff of experts under the Military Staff Committee, both the Security Council and the Secretary-General would have a single center to call on for professional military advice.

The Security Council should authorize the Committee: (1) to facilitate the preparation of special bilateral and multilateral agreements between the U.N. and the military contingents of member states; (2) to establish guidelines for such forces; (3) to develop a set of operating procedures for U.N. operations; (4) to initiate joint training exercises and programs for states participating in U.N. enforcement actions; (5) to coordinate logistic support and the equipment necessary in multinational operations; (6) to provide professional military staff support for the Security Council; and (7) to keep the Council and the Secretary-General informed and advised on military matters.

PEACEKEEPING

Regional organizations should be given a greater role in peace-building tasks, for example by establishing confidence-building measures among neighbors following a conflict. The risks inherent in having regional bodies or powers act as U.N. "deputies," however, mandate that any enforcement action they undertake be with the explicit consent of the Security Council.

Given the wide variety of contingencies for which U.N. forces are likely to be needed, a multi-tiered system of stand-by forces will be necessary to ensure adequate flexibility.

The **first tier** would be an immediately deployable, highly-skilled, volunteer force of 5,000-10,000 ground and airborne troops. Its primary mission would be deterrence and preemption as part of a larger strategy of preventive diplomacy, not long-term peacekeeping. It would be financed by a regular annual assessment.

The **second tier** would be a rapid deployment force numbering some 50,000-100,000, including air and naval support elements. This force would serve to deter major aggression or to turn back a lower-level aggression, and would be paid for by ad hoc assessments.

The **third tier** would be drawn from member states in the extreme case of a crisis with major global and regional repercussions requiring large-scale combat. This force could number well into the hundreds of thousands and would be paid for by the participating states and through special assessments of the whole U.N. membership.

The first two levels of these forces—those designated under Article 43—would conduct training exercises together on a regular basis, with operational command falling to officers of the nation contributing the largest portion of the forces and individual units remaining under a national commander within the overall integrated structure. The Secretary-General might be asked to recommend a commander for a particular operation, but he would not serve as the U.N.'s "commander-in-chief."

To accomplish the timely steps outlined above, the permanent members of the Security Council—especially the U.S. and Russia—must take the lead. Once it is accepted that the U.N. is the single best chance for securing a more orderly and principled international system, the establishment of U.N. enforcement capabilities will be seen as a logical step forward for Russia, America, and the world.

24
THE UNITED NATIONS &
WORLD ORDER

AMERICA SHOULD NOT GO TO WAR
FOR THE UNITED NATIONS

John McCain

John McCain is a United States Senator from Arizona.

Points to Consider:

1. What are the direct effects of conflict between the Executive Branch and Congress?

2. Explain the purpose of the Presidential Decision Directive known as PDD-13.

3. List and explain the four criteria the author proposes for United States involvement in foreign military intervention.

4. Why is the author opposed to committing United States forces to a standing army under the control of the United Nations?

5. How much does the United States currently spend on the military budget? Has spending declined or increased over the past ten years?

Excerpted from Congressional testimony by Senator John McCain before the House Government Operations Subcommittee on Legislation and National Security, March 3, 1994.

I am strongly opposed to committing U.S. forces to a standing army under the control of the U.N.

The tragic events in Somalia raised the issue of United States participation in United Nations peacekeeping operations to a matter of intense national interest. The Senate has since engaged in several deeply divided debates over the question of U.S. military participation in U.N. peacekeeping operations and, more importantly, our nation's rules of engagement for committing U.S. forces into harm's way in such operations. The escalation of tensions in Bosnia has heightened the urgency of reaching a consensus on a coherent, effective strategy for protecting U.S. interests and promoting U.S. values abroad amidst the confusion and challenges of a changing world.

Conflict between the Executive and Congress over the course of U.S. foreign policy is always a serious matter. It undermines the force of U.S. influence in the world, confuses our allies, and tempts our adversaries. The Administration could better avoid these troubling consequences by consulting more closely with Congress in formulating its policies.

CRITERIA FOR U.S. INVOLVEMENT

I opposed the deployment of U.S. forces in support of U.N.-led operations in Somalia, Haiti, and Bosnia. But my opposition in these instances does not mean that I would oppose any involvement of U.S. forces in international peacekeeping or peacemaking operations. Such involvement, however, like any American use of force, should be used sparingly, only when our vital interests coincide with other member nations; and only when the President of the United States determines that the use of American force is guided by the same criteria that govern our unilateral use of force.

First, the overriding rule against which the use of force must be measured is that of U.S. national interests. With few exceptions, American troops should not be ordered into conflict for any purpose unless our vital national interests are threatened, and unless all other means of protecting those interests have failed or are unavailable.

Second, there must be a clearly stated objective for the use of U.S. Armed Forces in conflict.

Third, the commitment of American soldiers must be of limited

150

Reprinted by permission: **Tribune Media Services.**

duration with a stated and achievable exit strategy. It is incumbent on the President to formulate and articulate a policy based on a realistic assessment of the risks involved and the prospects for success in protecting U.S. interests through the use of force. Then, the President must remain firmly committed to the military course of action throughout its duration.

Fourth, the reasons for sending U.S. troops into a conflict must be readily explainable to the American people, and a majority of public opinion should exist in support of the operation. The American people will demand a debate on any policy which may result in the dispatch of American troops, and they are right to do so.

We ought to be very clear, then, that the responsibilities incumbent on the American Commander-in-Chief who commits our forces to an enterprise are no different in a peacekeeping mission than they are when we use force to repel an attack on ourselves or our allies. Despite changes in the balance of forces in the world today, despite the emerging new threats to world peace and the variations on old ones, these responsibilities remain the most solemn duty of an American president, and they remain the President's alone.

151

THE ADMINISTRATION'S POLICY

The Clinton Administration was working to develop a Presidential Decision Directive known as PDD-13, with very little involvement by the Congress. That policy directive reportedly would have committed the U.S. to support multilateral peacekeeping and peacemaking operations politically, financially and militarily far more extensively than in the past and without direct control over the use of American troops in the operations.

The Administration announced a revised version of PDD-13 which makes significant progress away from the previous policy of "assertive multilateralism." The directive addresses a number of the major concerns raised by Congress, including some I have raised. It appears to recognize that it is in neither the U.S. interest nor the international community's to subject U.S. decision-making on grave matters of state, and the lives of American soldiers, to the frequently vacillating, contradictory, and reckless collective impulses of the United Nations.

U.S. FORCES

Some have argued that such a force is essential to the U.N.'s ability to respond swiftly and effectively to prevent conflicts in rapidly escalating situations around the world. I think such a force would encourage more misadventures like the peacekeeping *cum* peacemaking *cum* warlord-hunting operation in Somalia, where the lines of command are obscure and where ill-defined changes in the mission occur with every discussion in the Security Council. The Administration's policy appears to recognize these concerns.

I also have serious doubts about the wisdom of even considering a decision to place American troops under the operational command of foreign military personnel in a U.N.-led mission. The U.S. Armed Forces are the best trained, best equipped, most effective fighting force in the world. Our troops deserve the best leadership which is provided, more often than not, by American officers. This is not arrogance or elitism; it is simple fact.

RISING COSTS

Finally, with deficit reduction at the top of the Congress' and the Administration's agenda, the skyrocketing costs of U.N. peacekeeping operations should be a major cause of concern. According to the February 1994 issue of *Jane's Defense Weekly*, in 1992, the U.N. spent almost three times the amount spent in any prior year on peacekeeping operations. Last year, the cost doubled again to $3.6 billion. Charges of mismanagement and waste at the U.N. were so overwhelming that the Senate recently approved legislation to create an Inspector General at the United Nations.

To meet the U.S. share of these costs, which is set at 31.7 percent, the Administration proposes a greater burden on the Department of Defense. Defense spending has been declining steadily since 1985. By 1999, the defense budget will have been cut nearly 45 percent. Out of this shrinking budget, DOD will be assessed nearly $300 million in 1995 for U.N. peacekeeping operations, over and above the direct costs to the U.S. military of participating in some of these operations. The Department of Defense freely admits that this amount is insufficient to pay these costs, and the additional amounts will likely be taken from programs which actually contribute to the readiness of our military forces to protect our national security. This is an issue which will be closely scrutinized in the Armed Services Committees as we struggle to prioritize national security requirements within a severely constrained defense budget.

CONCLUSION

In the end, I believe my view is the common view shared by the majority of Americans. Committing American resources to a conflict—by which I mean the lives of American troops and the finances required to support them—is a national decision which should not be relegated or referred even in part to an international body.

25

THE UNITED NATIONS &
WORLD ORDER

THE CASE FOR A
UNITED NATIONS ARMY

Kai Bird

Kai Bird, a contributing editor of The Nation, *is the author of* The Chairman: John J. McCloy/The Making of the American Establishment.

Points to Consider:

1. What actions should be taken to prevent genocide?

2. How can the United States avoid playing the role of world supercop? What role should the United States play in foreign affairs?

3. Is the notion of forming an international army naive? Why or why not?

4. How could a United Nations army become merely an extension of United States national interests?

5. Describe what can be done now through existing institutions to respond to problems of genocide and starvation.

Kai Bird, "The Case for a U.N. Army," **The Nation**, August 8-15, 1994. This article is reprinted from **The Nation** magazine. © 1994 The Nation Company, L.P.

***Today, in the post-cold war era, I believe conflicts
approaching genocidal proportions demand collective
action.***

For good reason, most of us on the left have been anti-interven-
tionists. During the Vietnam era, I applied for and received status
as a conscientious objector. And yet, just a few years after the
end of the Vietnam War, as I witnessed in Lebanon the consequences of "ethnic cleansing," I began to wonder whether intervention of some sort might sometimes become a matter of simple
justice. Today, in the post-cold war era, I believe conflicts
approaching genocidal proportions demand collective action. As
a simple ethical imperative, genocide must be vigorously
opposed. At a minimum, instances of mass murder certainly call
for more nonviolent interventions—more aggressive diplomacy,
mediation and economic sanctions—but they may also require
multinational military intervention.

SUPERCOP

This doesn't mean the United States has to be the world's supercop, risking American troops to stop tribal warfare around the
globe. Any intervention should be conducted by an international
force under the auspices of the United Nations, which should start
developing a sizable, standing U.N. army with troops from around
the globe. Eventually, this international army should be a credible
force, capable of shutting down the frenzied killing fields of a
Rwanda, say, in a matter of days.

Under the present U.N. charter, such a standing U.N. army
would have to receive its orders from the Security Council, so we
should not expect that it would be intervening in every ethnic
conflict. Obviously, the present Security Council system is highly
publicized, and dominated by the concerns of a few large powers,
especially the United States. No doubt the United States would
use its veto power to block some humanitarian interventions, say
in East Timor. This would be an outrageous abuse of power, but
perhaps also politically embarrassing. Still, if there were a standing U.N. army, at least there would be the possibility of acting, of
saving some lives, when the international community could reach
a consensus. (And over time, we should work toward reforming
the U.N. system to make it more democratic and less an instrument of great-power diplomacy.)

U.N. ARMY

Is the notion of an international army completely naive? Before joining the Administration, Clinton's own Defense Secretary, William Perry, wrote an essay arguing for just such a "multinational expeditionary force," together with "a major restructuring and down-sizing" of the U.S. military. Now that he is inside the Administration, Perry claims that world circumstances make such a multilateral force politically impossible. Clearly, he is expressing the Administration's view, which simply reflects the strong opposition in this country to the whole concept of international peacekeeping forces. But this has not slowed the long-term, inexorable trend toward increasing reliance on the U.N. to deal with such problems. With seventeen current U.N. peacekeeping forces already in place, it is clear that we are seeing the haphazard creation of an embryonic international army.

The U.N. intervention in Somalia became messy in part because the U.S. forces involved had such a high political profile. But the intervention itself saved thousands upon thousands of Somalis who otherwise would have starved. The blatant genocide in Rwanda demanded intervention by the international community, and a similar case for humanitarian intervention can be made in Angola, where the United States for years supported Jonas Savimbi's Unita forces, and where the U.N. is today playing an entirely ineffective role. Such crises demonstrate why the U.N. must be given a standing army authorized to intervene for narrowly specified periods—a few months, perhaps—to stop mass killings. The U.N. need not get into the business of "nation-building," but it can create the limited armistices necessary to allow armed adversaries the chance to negotiate political agreements. This is being attempted with some success by the U.N. today in Cambodia.

MANIPULATION

It is also true, as Noam Chomsky and Richard Falk argued in essays in the December/January *Boston Review*, that the U.N. itself has been manipulated by the United States in ways that make a mockery of the whole notion of humanitarian interventions. A standing U.N. army could become merely an extension of narrowly defined U.S. national interests. But both Chomsky and Falk conclude that this does not answer the question of whether there are nevertheless good reasons for the interventions

Reprinted with permission from **Star Tribune**, Minneapolis.

that are now being debated. "That is a separate matter," Chomsky writes, "to be faced without illusions about our unique nobility." Even Falk, who is convinced that the case against intervention remains "virtually unconditional," concludes that "in the face of massacre and genocide there should be no hard-and-fast rules that preclude response."

So, what should be done now? At the moment, we lack a U.N. army, and the politics of peacekeeping—both past and present— are so muddied that we cannot expect an international army to emerge overnight. What can be done now through existing institutions to respond to mass murder?

First, it is essential to call things by their right names. In each of these countries—Haiti, Bosnia, Rwanda and Angola—mass slaughter has been committed, often for reasons of "ethnic cleansing," or, in the case of Haiti, class warfare by a small elite against the masses. Such actions are a reversion to fascism, and we on the left should insist that these crimes against defenseless civilians be thoroughly investigated and documented in a judicial fashion.

Second, given the unbearable choice of standing passively in the face of genocide or risking the kind of intervention that we know historically has frequently been only a cover for advancing

157

U.S. hegemony, we should be raising our voices in support of a foreign policy that is based on a broad definition of human rights. Where appropriate—meaning where we believe mass murders or genocide or "ethnic cleansing" is occurring—we should urge a policy of principled, multinational intervention, to be conducted through the U.N.

Finally, in the absence of an effective U.N. intervention force or an international criminal court, we must be willing to risk making some judgments in those situations where the crimes of mass murder are so clear that even some form of unilateral intervention is demanded. At that point, we should be willing to urge upon our own government those kinds of interventions we might otherwise support only if we did indeed have an effective U.N., an international army and an international criminal court. We must, in other words, sometimes try to act as if the world had an international judicial system.

Skeptics will argue that sanctions can never be made airtight, and that the threat of international indictments against warlords is hardly believable. This may seem true today, but in the decades to come, it need not be the case if we begin now to create new legal instruments for humanitarian intervention. The world community needs to make pariahs of people like those in Bosnia, Haiti, Rwanda and Angola who are responsible for mass murders; to withhold—and block—all forms of aid and arms exports to murderous governments and military establishments (and their civilian beneficiaries); and to show that some day these leaders may well be brought to justice. If the United States and the rest of the world can establish a precedent for dealing with thugs like Lieut. Gen. Raoul Cédras of Haiti and Slobodan Milosevic of Serbia, perhaps—just perhaps—other fascists will be deterred.

THE UNITED NATIONS & WORLD ORDER

THE CASE AGAINST A UNITED NATIONS ARMY

George F. Will

George F. Will is a nationally syndicated columnist. He is a leading spokesman for conservative ideas.

Points to Consider:

1. What role should the United States play in a standing United Nations military force?

2. Why does the author oppose a standing United Nations army?

3. In regard to military intervention, what is the relationship between individual vs. collective security among nations?

4. Explain the United Nations Participation Act of 1945.

5. What is the basic premise of Article 43?

Article 43 authorizes a standing U.N. military force. But now such a force may be a bad idea whose time has come.

The United States has passed a milestone on the descending path to diluted sovereignty and, hence, to the diminished relevance of its representative institutions.

Thousands of U.S. troops were placed under United Nations command, exercised by a Turkish general. Never before has there been foreign command of U.S. military units. But that could become common if U.N. Secretary General Boutros Boutros-Ghali and various U.S. politicians have their way with Article 43 of the U.N. Charter.

STANDING FORCE

Article 43 authorizes a standing U.N. military force. The Cold War paralysis of the United Nations fortunately prevented creation of such a force. But now such a force may be a bad idea whose time has come.

The Senate Foreign Relations Committee endorsed it. Candidate Clinton said the United States should consider the merits of a "standby, voluntary U.N. rapid deployment force." Before James Woolsey became Clinton's CIA director, he led a study group for the United Nations Association of the United States which endorsed having nations provide the U.N. with troops for three sorts of military forces.

But when Les Aspin was being confirmed as Secretary of Defense he said, "The President is Commander in Chief...Congress has war powers. And if you second these forces to the U.N., how do you maintain the Constitution?" Good question.

The Korean War and, 40 years later, the Gulf War were approved but not controlled by the U.N. Regarding Korea, all the Security Council did was declare North Korea's aggression illegal and ask members to help South Korea. Although Gen. MacArthur commanded "U.N. forces," 90 percent of the non-South Korean forces were American, and MacArthur never reported to the Security Council. It had nothing to do with major decisions, such as crossing the 38th parallel or refusing forcible repatriation of prisoners.

Cartoon by Bob Gorrell. Reprinted with permission of **Copley News Service**.

In the Gulf War in 1991-92, the U.S.-led coalition used the U.N. to burnish collective security. But as Eugene Rostow, professor of law and diplomacy, notes, the Security Council did not even meet between Nov. 29, 1990, and Feb. 16, 1991, the period of maximum violence.

INDIVIDUAL VS. COLLECTIVE SECURITY

Article 51 of the charter affirms each nation's right to individual or collective self-defense and was the basis of the U.N.'s Aug. 2, 1990, response to Iraq's invasion of Kuwait. But as Rostow says, Article 51 is in tension with Article 43. On Article 43 rest the extravagant aspirations of Boutros-Ghali and the equally extravagant hopes of those Americans who think the U.N. could relieve the United States of the burdens of being the only superpower.

Unfortunately, Article 43 is the law of the land—our land.

On Oct. 21, 1944, President Franklin Roosevelt said, "The Council of the United Nations must have the power to act quickly and decisively to keep the peace by force, if necessary." In the fourth and final draft of that speech he crossed out this sentence: "We shall enter a peace organization as a sovereign power, and therefore, our representative in that organization cannot legislate for us."

Then came the United Nations Participation Act of 1945. It

U.N. POLICE FORCE

For some time, U.N. Secretary General Boutros Boutros-Ghali has advocated a radical transformation of the whole purpose and scope of the United Nations.

He wants the organization to acquire its own independent military and police force. His idea would change the United Nations from an assembly of sovereign nations whose delegates reflect the wishes of their governments and people to an independent and supranational power that gives orders to nations.

Samuel Francis, "U.N. Could Be the World's Next Superpower," **Tribune Media Services,** Inc., 1992.

says that Congress shall be involved in endorsing whatever the President negotiates by way of allotments of military forces to Security Council control, but "the President shall not be deemed to require the authorization of the Congress to make available to the Security Council on its call" those military forces whose availability has been previously negotiated.

On Sept. 19, 1944, Sen. Joseph Ball, R-Minn., expressed the dominant mood of that era: "The question raised here by several senators is whether even such a United States quota force should be used to stop aggression at the direction of the [U.N.] council, our representative agreeing, unless Congress had formally declared war...I cannot see how the constitutional authority of Congress to declare war is concerned in the slightest. The world security organization would not be making war, but preserving the peace."

Please. No such sophistry now. War waged to stop aggression is war nonetheless.

ARTICLE 43

Rostow argues against resuscitating Article 43 because the system of nation states has not "evolved" sufficiently. That is, nations "are not confident enough" of one another to surrender or even qualify their right to self-defense, which is the essence of sovereignty. What Rostow does not say but what should be said is this: Such an evolution would not be progress. Sovereignty is linked

162

with liberty under representative government.

Government's most serious decision is to send its military in harm's way. Nothing would so seriously derogate American representative government than the allocation of American forces to non-American control for missions not chosen by persons directly accountable to American voters. Therefore, events may yet compel a reconsideration, and, perhaps in Bosnia, repeal, of aspects of the U.N. Participation Act of 48 years ago.

INTERPRETING EDITORIAL CARTOONS

This activity may be used as an individualized study guide for students in libraries and resource centers or as a discussion catalyst in small group and classroom discussions.

Although cartoons are usually humorous, the intent of most political cartoonists is not to entertain. Cartoons express serious social comment about important issues. Using graphic and visual arts, the cartoonist expresses opinions and attitudes. By employing an entertaining and often light-hearted visual format, cartoonists may have as much or more impact on national and world issues as editorial and syndicated columnists.

Points to Consider:

1. Examine the cartoon on Page 151.

2. How would you describe the message of the cartoon? Try to describe the message in one to three sentences.

3. Do you agree with the message expressed in the cartoon? Why or why not?

4. Does the cartoon support the author's point of view in any of the readings in this publication? If the answer is yes, be specific about which reading or readings and why.

5. Are any of the readings in Chapter Five in basic agreement with the cartoon?

BIBLIOGRAPHY

Humanitarian Intervention

Albright, M. K. "Explanation of U.S. vote on lifting arms embargo against Bosnia" [statement, June 29, 1993], **U.S. Department of State Dispatch** v4 (July 5, 1993): p479.

"Bosnian sides find a new weapon: food," **Time** v141 (March 1, 1993): p11-12.

"Eyewitness Rwanda," **Life** v17 (Summer 1994): p74-80.

Goose, S. D. and F. Smyth. "Arming genocide in Rwanda," **Foreign Affairs** v73 (September/October 1994): p86-96.

Hanson, C. "Courting disaster" [reporting from refugee camp in Goma, Zaire], **Columbia Journalism Review** v33 (September/October 1994): p49.

Jenkins, S. "Rwanda's agony: can horrors be prevented? No: and more aid can only hurt," **World Press Review** v41 (September 1994): p11-12.

"Inside Srebrenica: city of the damned," **Newsweek** v121 (April 12, 1993): p40-1.

Meron, T. "The case for war crimes trials in Yugoslavia," **Foreign Affairs** v72 (Summer 1993): p122-35.

Montgomery, M. "Flight of terror: Muslim refugees die in a stampede for places on a U.N. convoy" [town of Srebrenica], **Time** v 141 (April 12, 1993): p38-9.

Nelan, B. W. "A convert among the dying" [General P. Morillon of the U.N. peace force stands in with Muslim refugees caught in siege of Srebrenica], **Time** v141 (March 29, 1993): p39.

Parker, R. A. "Ten hours in Rwanda," **The New Yorker** v70 (October 17, 1994): p92-3.

Purvis, A. "Collusion with killers" [aid supplies co-opted by members of former government], **Time** v144 (November 7, 1994): p52.

Signy, H. "A well-planned extermination," **World Press Review** v41 (September 1994): p14-15.

Silberger, K. "Will war crimes go unpunished?" (resolution passed by United Nations Security Council], **Ms.** v4 (July/August 1993): p26-7.

Peacekeeping

Albright, M. K. "Shared resolve in restoring democracy in Haiti" [statement and text of Resolution 940, July 31, 1994], **U.S. Department of State Dispatch** v5 (August 15, 1994): p554-6.

Albright, M. K. "The tragedy in Rwanda: international cooperation to find a solution" [statement and Security Council Resolution 929, June 22, 1994], **U.S. Department of State Dispatch** v5 (June 27, 1994): p438-9.

Bilski, A. "The siege of Haiti" [U.N. Security Council authorizes U.S.-led invasion], **Maclean's** v107 (August 15, 1994): p16-17.

Bird, K. "The case for a U.N. army," **The Nation** v259 (August 8-15, 1994): p160+.

Caragata, W. "Making a difference" (U.N. peacekeeping mission; interview with Major General R. Dallaire], **Maclean's** v107 (September 19, 1994): p32.

Cleveland, H. "Ten keys to world peace," **The Futurist** v28 (July/August 1994): p15-17+.

"Goodwill missions" [increasing U.N.'s role in humanitarian emergencies], **National Review** v46 (August 29, 1994): p19-20.

Isaacs, J. D. "A confederation of caution" [U.S. involvement in U.N. peacekeeping operations], **The Bulletin of the Atomic Scientists** v50 (July/August 1994): p14-15.

Kirkpatrick, J. J. "Clinton's real mistake in Somalia," **Reader's Digest** v144 (January 1994): p55-8.

Lummis, C. D. "Time to watch the watchers" [U.N. generating criminal law; cover story], **The Nation** v259 (September 26, 1994): p302-4+.

Martin, I. "Haiti: mangled multilateralism," **Foreign Policy** v95 (Summer 1994): p72-89.

Peach, K. "Cambodia's new killing field" [AIDS victims include U.N. personnel], **World Press Review** v41 (January 1994): p40-1.

Talbott, S. and J. M. Deutch. "U.S.-CARICOM efforts to support U.N. Security Council Resolution 940" [remarks, August 31, 1994], **U.S. Department of State Dispatch** v5 (September 5, 1994): p589-91.

"U.N. Security Council adopts Resolution 918 on Rwanda," **U.S. Department of State Dispatch** v5 (May 30, 1994): p352-3.

Weinberger, C. W. "How to lose a 'peacekeeping force'," **Forbes** v154 (August 29, 1994): p33.

Wittes, B. "The politics of peacekeeping," **The New Leader** v77 (May 9-23, 1994): p10-11.

Wright, R. "Good Ghali" [air support and lifting the Bosnia arms embargo], **The New Republic** v211 (August 15, 1994): p6.

Intervention and the United Nations

Albright, M. K. "A strong United Nations serves U.S. security interests" [address, June 11, 1993], **U.S. Department of State Dispatch** v4 (June 28, 1993): p461-4.

Albright, M. K. "Building a consensus on international peace-keeping" [statement, October 20, 1993], **U.S. Department of State Dispatch** v4 (November 15, 1993): p789-92.

Bloomfield, L. P. "Policing world disorder," **World Monitor** v6 (February 1993): p34-7.

Boutrous-Ghali, B. "Empowering the United Nations," **Foreign Affairs** v71 (Winter 1992/1993): p89-102.

Di Rita, L. T. "C'mon, baby–do the multilalteral" (Clinton administration], **National Review** v45 (October 4, 1993): p42-4.

"Enforcing human rights: the U.N. machinery," **UN Chronicle** v30 (March 1993): p93-4.

Hughes, D. "U.N. tracking weapon deliveries," **Aviation Week & Space Technology** v139 (November 22, 1993): p94.

Lefever, E. W. "Reining in the U.N.: mistaking the instrument for the actor," **Foreign Affairs** v72 (Summer 1993): p17-20.

Maynes, C. W. "Containing ethnic conflict," **Foreign Policy** v90 (Spring 1993): p3-21.

Mayor, F. "War and peace in the minds of men," **The Unesco Courier** v46 (March 1993): p44-5.

McMullen, R. K. and A. R. Norton. "Somalia and other adventures for the 1990s" [political upheavals in weak states], **Current History** v92 (April 1993): p169-74.

Michaels, M. "Blue-helmet blues," **Time** v142 (November 15, 1993): p66-7.

O'Sullivan, J. "On the beach" [United Nations and U.S. foreign policy], **National Review** v45 (January 18, 1993): p6.

Stedman, S. J. "The new interventionists," **Foreign Affairs** v72 Special Issue (1993): p1-16.

Stedman, S. J. "The new interventionists: civil wars and human rights," **Current** (Washington, D.C.) v354 (July/August 1993): p34-40.

"The new jingoes" [views of Stephen John Stedman], **The Wilson Quarterly** v17 (Spring 1993): p130-2.

Urquhart, B. E. "For a UN volunteer military force" [cover story], **The New York Review of Books** v40 (June 10, 1993): p3-4.

Wright, R. "Bold old vision" [collective security], **The New Republic** v208 (January 25, 1993): p19-20+.

Iraq

Fulghum, D. A. "Allies strike Iraq for defying U.N.," **Aviation Week & Space Technology** v138 (January 18, 1993): p22-3+.

"Full compliance with resolutions asked," **UN Chronicle** v30 (March 1993) p17-20.

Kay, D. A. "Bomb shelter" [U.N. weapons inspection of Iraq], **The New Republic** v208 (March 15, 1993): p11-13.

Milhollin, G. "The Iraqi bomb," **The New Yorker** v68 (February 1, 1993): p47-54+.

Mirkarimi, R. and S. Zaidi. "Iraq: sanctioned suffering," **Ms.** v3 (March/April 1993): p14.

Stahel, T. H. "Iraq and the United Nations" [interview with R. Ekéus], **America** v169 (August 14-21, 1993): p4-5.

Somalia

Bilski, A. "On the attack" [U.N. peacekeepers retaliate for deaths of 23 Pakistani soldiers], **Maclean's** v106 (June 28, 1993): p18-19.

Krauthammer, C. "The immaculate intervention," **Time** v142 (July 26, 1993): p78.

Masland, T. "The pitfalls of peacekeeping," **Newsweek** v122 (July 26, 1993): p32-3.

Michaels, M. "Peacemaking war," **Time** v142 (July 26, 1993): p48.

Nemeth, M. "Somali fiasco" [U.N. air attack], **Maclean's** v106 (July 26, 1993): p20-1.

Thomas, E. "Playing globocop" [bombing of Somali warlord's compound raises questions concerning America's world role], **Newsweek** v121 (June 28, 1993): p20-4.